Ely Cathedral Design and Meaning

John Maddison

Ely Cathedral Publications

The Dean and Chapter of Ely acknowledges with gratitude generous assistance from Rattee & Kett, the Friends of Ely Cathedral and the Idlewild Trust in the production of this volume.

ACKNOWLEDGEMENTS

I have had a great deal of help in the writing of this book. First of all, I must thank the Dean and Chapter for commissioning it and also those organisations which have generously contributed towards the costs of the publication. Then there are those who have readily made time to read part or all of the manuscript: Ian Atherton, Thomas Cocke, Peter Cormack, Philip Dixon, Eric Fernie, John Inge, Simon Keynes, Phillip Lindley and Peter Meadows. It was much improved by their advice and in places helpfully restrained. Some of them are contributors to an important volume of scholarly essays on the cathedral and its history that is being prepared at the time of writing.

I have also had useful information, ideas and practical help from Tony Baggs, Sarah Bayliss, Pamela Blakeman, Gill Cannell, Sandra Coley, Paul Crossley, John Heward, Jacques Heyman, Anne Holton-Krayenbuhl, Edward Maddison, Zara Matthews, Bridget Nicholls, David Park, Gavin Simpson, David Smout and Ella Thurmot. I am grateful to Janet Fairweather for making available the longer passages from the *Liber Eliensis* in advance of her forthcoming translation. The cathedral vergers have been unfailingly helpful with requests for keys, access and other forms of assistance. Credits for photographs other than my own are given in the captions but I owe a special debt to Philip Dixon, the Cathedral's Consultant Archaeologist, whose skill with the plate camera will be evident to all. Jenny Knight's expert and sympathetic copy editing has been invaluable. Tim McPhee has produced a handsome design while Tracey Smith and Hilary MacCallum have seen the whole enterprise through the press with efficiency, patience and good humour.

The quotation from Archbishop Wulfstan on page 9 is reprinted by permission of Everyman's Library and the extract on page 83 from the Rule of St Benedict is reprinted by permission of Gracewing Publishing. Figure 58 is reproduced by kind permission from *English Historic Carpentry*, by Cecil A. Hewett, published in 1980 by Phillimore and Co Ltd, Shopwyke Manor Barn, Chichester, West Sussex. The picture of the funeral of Bishop Cox in 1581 *(Col. pl. 13)* appears by permission of the Lord Bishop of Ely and the Church Commissioners.

Finally, I have to thank my wife, Jane Kennedy, the Surveyor to the Fabric. She has put up with a lot, especially during the last year. Her intimate knowledge of the building and sound judgement have been indispensable.

THE AUTHOR

John Maddison undertook a research degree on medieval buildings before serving as Architectural Advisor to the Victorian Society, and then Historic Buildings Representative to the National Trust in East Anglia. He is now a practising artist who continues to write and lecture on architectural history. He sits on a number of committees connected with the care of ancient buildings, is a Fellow of the Society of Antiquaries and a member of the cathedral congregation.

Published by Ely Cathedral Publications
© 2000 John Maddison
All rights reserved. No part of this publication may be reproduced, stored in any retrieval system or transmitted in any form or by any means, electronic, mechanical, photocopying, recording or otherwise, without prior written permission of the copyright holder to which application should be addressed in the first instance.

A CIP catalogue record for this book is available from the British Library.
ISBN 1 873027 03 6

Design and production in association with
Book Production Consultants plc, 25–27 High Street, Chesterton, Cambridge CB4 1ND, UK
http://www.bpccam.co.uk
Printed and bound by St Edmundsbury Press, Suffolk

CONTENTS

ELY CATHEDRAL

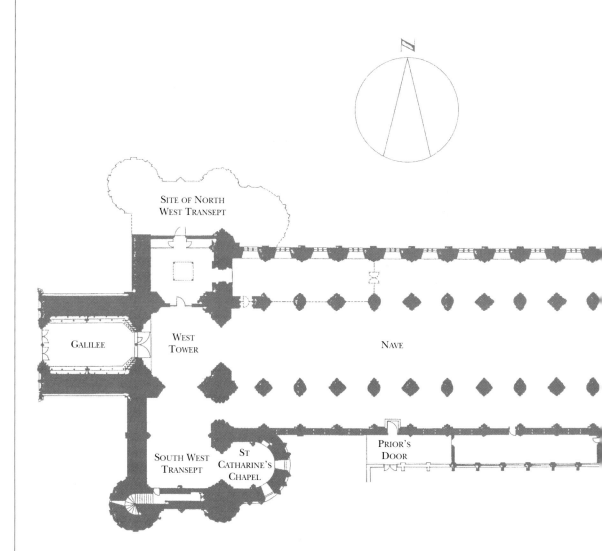

SITE OF NORTH
WEST TRANSEPT

GALILEE

WEST
TOWER

NAVE

SOUTH WEST
TRANSEPT

ST
CATHARINE'S
CHAPEL

PRIOR'S
DOOR

PLAN 1

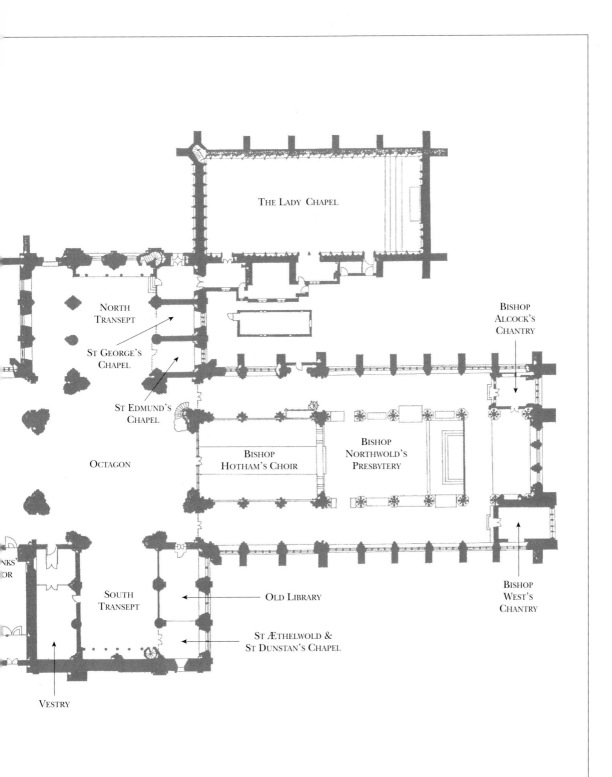

THE LADY CHAPEL

NORTH TRANSEPT

ST GEORGE'S CHAPEL

ST EDMUND'S CHAPEL

OCTAGON

BISHOP ALCOCK'S CHANTRY

BISHOP HOTHAM'S CHOIR

BISHOP NORTHWOLD'S PRESBYTERY

SOUTH TRANSEPT

OLD LIBRARY

BISHOP WEST'S CHANTRY

ST ÆTHELWOLD & ST DUNSTAN'S CHAPEL

VESTRY

NKS' OR

PREFACE

More than once during the writing of this book I have been asked whether it will contain anything new or whether it will merely summarise what is already known. Since the eighteenth century there has been a gradual succession of significant studies of the cathedral, each increasing our understanding and quickening our admiration of this intriguing and beautiful building. The picture to which these works have contributed is however far from complete and will never be comprehensive. There is much that we can never hope to rediscover but there is still a great deal to be learnt by looking carefully at the building.

Those who know the cathedral well – long-standing members of the community and congregation – will readily acknowledge that in spite of daily contact, it never becomes entirely familiar. The building is its own history. It is like a lengthy and much thumbed compilation written in an old language, a text from which some pages have been torn and to which other gatherings have been added, with some passages rubbed out and partially or wholly rewritten. No one could master it completely and yet everyone who visits the cathedral and looks at it carefully reads parts of this ancient text. The design, shape, texture and colour of the stones; the marks of lost timbers, pieces of carved decoration, fragments of paint and imagery both obvious and obscure – all these signs are there for everyone to examine and interpret. Each individual either sees or looks for something different. We carry our own preoccupations with us and it goes without saying that no one today will approach the building in the same frame of mind as any of our ancestors. This book therefore suggests some of the ways in which the great church and its people have been understood, revered or reviled at different times in its history. It is hoped that these ideas will encourage others to return to the cathedral and read the building for themselves.

1. (left) The south transept, begun in 1081.

1. ETHELDREDA AND ANGLO-SAXON ELY:
Light and Darkness

Etheldreda and her family. The foundation of the monastery in 672 and her death seven years later. The translation of her body into the church in 694. The miracles and the significance of the Etheldreda story. Ely is destroyed by the Danes in 869. Æthelwold and Dunstan re-establish the monastery and introduce the Rule of St Benedict in 970. Descriptions of the contents of the Saxon church and evidence of its architectural character.

Ely lies in the province of the East Angles, an area of about six hundred hides ... it resembles an island surrounded by water and marshes, and derives its name from the vast quantity of eels that are caught in the marshes. And the servant of Christ wished to have her monastery in this place

Bede's Ecclesiastical History of the English People, 731

THE SAINT

Etheldreda is the Latin name of Ely's founding saint and the one that we use today. In the later Middle Ages, they found it easier to call her Audrey. Her real name was, however, Æthelthryth. It is rarely used now and pronounced only with difficulty: a measure of the thirteen hundred years that lie between our

2. (left) Something of the character of the ancient Fenland is preserved at Wicken.

time and hers. For more than eight hundred years the shrine of Etheldreda lay behind the high altar of the great church at Ely and was central to its power and prestige. Etheldreda's miracle-working relics attracted pilgrims in large numbers and were the inspiration for one of the great architectural compositions of medieval Europe.

To put aside the ancient splendours of the cathedral and enter an even more remote period when organised Christianity in Britain was both new and relatively precarious requires an effort of imagination. Etheldreda's Anglo-Saxon ancestors came as pagan raiders in the closing years of the Roman Empire. After 410, when the legions were finally withdrawn, they settled. The earlier inhabitants were driven before them and what remained of Romano-British Christianity retreated into the Celtic west. Gradually pagan Europe was converted by Roman papal missionaries who saw themselves as the heirs and restorers of the fallen empire. Pope Gregory the Great sent Augustine to

Britain, where he was received in 597 by the Kentish king, Ethelbert. With Ethelbert's help, the Christian message was spread further afield. According to a later account, a church was built then at Ely on or near the site of the cathedral.

At first, the pagans had difficulty grasping the exclusive claims of the new faith. Bede tells the story of Etheldreda's great-uncle, Redwald, who is thought to be the subject of the famous ship burial at Sutton Hoo. He 'tried to serve both Christ and the ancient gods', having 'in the same shrine an altar for the holy Sacrifice of Christ side by side with a small altar on which victims were offered to devils'. Redwald's more committed Christian successors were continu-

ally at war with the pagan Mercians. Local tradition maintains that in 637 they destroyed the church at Ely founded in c.600. In this war the great warrior king Sigeberht, who had set aside his crown, renounced soldiery and entered a monastery, was compelled by his followers to fight one last battle. His new faith denied him the use of his trusted weapons and he died, one of Christ's soldiers, brandishing a wooden staff. The death of Sigeberht and his cousin King Ecric made way for a new East Anglian king, Anna. He is described by Bede as 'a good man … blessed with good and holy children'. Anna's four holy daughters, Ethelburga, Etheldreda, Sexburga and Withburga, are the beginning of

3. Three relief sculptures from the octagon (1322–8): (above left) Etheldreda grieving over the body of her first husband, Tondberht. (above right) Etheldreda's staff, planted in the ground, sends forth naturalistic ash leaves and fruits while she sleeps. (below left) Etheldreda's death and translation. Her miraculously intact body is placed in a Roman sarcophagus fourteen years after her death. (below right) Roman sarcophagus similar to the one shown in the fourteenth-century relief and found in 1981 at Stuntney near Ely. (By permission of the trustees of the Ely Museum)

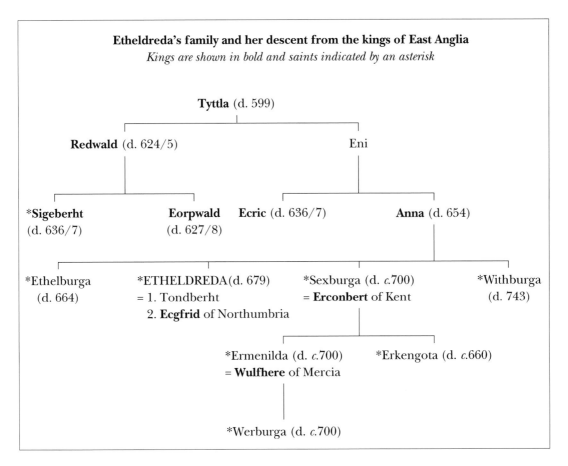

Etheldreda's family and her descent from the kings of East Anglia

Kings are shown in bold and saints indicated by an asterisk

our story. Etheldreda was born not far from Ely, at Exning near Newmarket.

The main events in Etheldreda's life were illustrated in the fourteenth century in a series of sculpted reliefs fitted into the corners of the great octagon which forms the centre of Ely cathedral *(Fig. 3)*. In the mid-fifteenth century certain events were depicted in some magnificent painted panels *(Col. pl. 11)*. Initially, it seemed that she was destined to be an instrument of political consolidation. She was married off first to a prince, Tondberht, leader of the fen people called the South Gyrwas, but he died before the marriage had been consummated. The monks of Ely were later to assert that the Isle of Ely was Tondberht's marriage gift to Etheldreda. In 660 her second marriage, to Ecgfrid, king of Northumbria, secured a power-

ful allegiance and brought her into the orbit of Northumbrian Christianity. The king was then a boy but even after twelve years, according to Bede, in spite of her husband's protests, Etheldreda 'preserved the glory of perpetual virginity'. She left him and entered the convent at Coldingham in 672, receiving the veil from her spiritual mentor Bishop Wilfred.

Wilfred was Bede's principal source for the details of Etheldreda's life and a central figure in the early development of English Christianity. He had established the pre-eminence of Roman practice over the native Celtic Christian tradition at the Synod of Whitby in 664. His influence will have affected the way in which Etheldreda practised her faith, but she already had family links with established Christian communities in Gaul. In about 660 one of her nieces, Erkengota, died at her aunt Ethelburga's double monastery of Faremoutier-en-Brie. The appearance of angelic beings on the eve of Erkengota's death, and the fact that her grave exhaled a sweet balsam-like odour, showed that a new saint had entered the calendar. In 664 Etheldreda's sister, Sexburga, had become a widow and had taken the veil in the monastery which she had founded at Sheppey. In 671, the year before she herself took the veil, Etheldreda would have learnt of a second family miracle. The body of her sister Ethelburga, after seven years in a temporary grave, was translated to a church near Faremoutier and found to be incorrupt, a sure sign of her sanctity and virginity. So Etheldreda's response to the call of the cloister and her subsequent ascent to sainthood formed part of an established pattern.

She remained at Coldingham for a year before travelling back to her own country in East Anglia, initially hotly pursued by her husband. The miraculous events that attended this journey are described in the twelfth-century *Liber Eliensis*, a massive compilation which incorporates a good deal of lost pre-Conquest material and is the principal source for the history of Ely before 1150. Because it was written to protect the possessions of the monastery and to attest the authenticity and power of Ely's saints, it is not an entirely objective account. It is, however, a valuable record of history as it was understood by the monks. But if we rely on Bede's much earlier history we find that in 673 Etheldreda

was herself made Abbess in the district called Ely, where she built a convent and became the virgin mother of many virgins vowed to God and displayed the pattern of heavenly life in word and deed ... She was taken to Christ in the presence of her nuns, seven years after her appointment as abbess, and in accordance with her instructions she was buried among them in the wooden coffin in which she died.

Etheldreda's death on 23 June 679 was for her a welcome transition to eternal life. She bore her final illness with gladness, and regarded the painful swelling on her neck (a symptom of bubonic plague) as a God-given penance for the vanity of wearing too much jewellery as a girl. Her contemporary, Aldhelm (639–709), concludes his treatise on virginity with a warning against splendid clothing and jewels. The grave goods of other post-conversion Saxons moreover suggest that at this time the complex Germanic necklaces were being given up in favour of the simplicity of Roman fashions. Examples of the old necklaces, made of brilliantly coloured glass beads, have been excavated at a large pagan cemetery south of Ely.

The writer of the *Liber Eliensis* believed that Etheldreda built her monastery around the remains of the church built in Augustine's time. 'And as soon as it was rebuilt, dedicated, as of old, in honour of Mary the holy Mother of God, it became a shining light, through innumerable signs and miracles, as God carried out His work every day.' The main settlement of Ely, he explained, was situated a mile away at Cratendune, a low-lying place which may prove to be the large and complex site excavated on the western edge of the city in 1999. The position of the church and monastery, near the river, was by contrast one of the highest points of the continuous sickle-shaped plateau that forms the Isle of Ely.

Because the great drainage campaigns of the seventeenth century turned the Fens into high-quality farmland, it is not easy to visualise the watery and swamp-like character of the terrain before that date. An area of surviving fen preserved by the National Trust at Wicken (*Fig. 2*) gives in places some idea of the landscape in Etheldreda's time. It was impassable to anyone without detailed local knowledge and, except in times of drought or severe frost, it presented conditions of exceptional difficulty for large armies. The well-drained and fertile southern slopes of the isle, however, made it ideal for settlement and for the establishment of monastic life.

The first translation of Etheldreda's body

In 694, fourteen years after Etheldreda's death, her sister, the abbess Sexburga, exhumed Etheldreda's body and moved it into the church. Ely, like Faremoutier, was a double monastery for monks and nuns, and the brothers were sent out to find stone for a coffin. A masonry coffin was necessary because Etheldreda was to be 'elevated', that is entombed above ground to indicate her exalted spiritual status. Bede relates:

> And since the district of Ely was surrounded on all sides by sea and fens and had no large stones, they took boat and came to a small ruined city not far distant which the English call Grantacaestir [Cambridge]. After a short while they discovered near the city walls a white marble sarcophagus of very beautiful workmanship with a close-fitting lid of similar stone; and realising that God had prospered their journey, they returned thanks to him and brought it back to the convent.

The use of the second-hand sarcophagus was part of the growing regard for all things Roman. It was so widespread in Gaul that a decree was issued to stop the looting of Roman coffins to provide shrines for saints. The old Roman city of Cambridge would have been used as a quarry since at least the early fifth century. No one would therefore have been surprised to see the brothers rummaging in its extra-mural cemetery and then loading the heavy sarcophagus onto the creaking timbers of their boat. But this was a momentous occasion; it was the beginning of the cult of St Etheldreda.

Bede now recounts the important miracles that made Etheldreda a saint. A tent was erected over the burial site. Today this would be associated with a forensic investigation but in the Etheldreda tradition it is the earliest example of the secrecy which surrounds the miracle of her incorrupt body. Those who were privileged to enter, including her physician Cynifrid, 'saw the body of the holy virgin taken from its grave and laid on a bed as though asleep', and noted that the swelling had disappeared. Her linen clothes looked fresh and new. Touching them had the effect of casting out devils, while the wood of her coffin cured blindness. The sarcophagus was exactly the right size in every dimension.

The legend of the sprouting staff

Bede mentions no miracles during the lifetime of the saint but the *Liber Eliensis* makes good this deficiency with a remarkable occurrence during her flight from Northumbria. She had paused to sleep on a grassy bank somewhere in Lincolnshire and when she awoke her ash staff, which she had driven into the ground, had burst into leaf while she slept. A willow branch will still perform this feat today, especially in the moist earth of the Fens, though not quite so quickly. This was, however, a deeply symbolic event, and one that should be interpreted as a demonstration of Etheldreda's virginity and a confirmation of her calling. In Numbers 17.8 the sprouting of Aaron's staff fulfilled God's promise that 'the staff of the man which I choose will put forth buds'. Isaiah (11.1) prophesied 'there shall come forth a rod out of the stem of Jesse, and a branch shall grow out of his roots', and the Latin word for 'rod' (*virga*) was readily associated in the medieval mind with the word for 'virgin' (*virgo*). The early legends of the Church accordingly associated the miraculous sprouting staff with two prominent saints noted for their chastity: Joseph, the foster father of Christ, and Christopher.

The *Liber Eliensis* implicitly invites its readers to discover these parallels. Christopher's staff sprouted after he had waded through a river bearing the Christ Child on his shoulders and Etheldreda's sprouted after she had crossed the Humber. Other comparisons would have been obvious to contemporary readers. Her escape from the pursuing Ecgfrid, who was cut off by a high tide at St Abb's Head, would certainly have brought to mind the deliverance of the Israelites in the Red Sea.

Medieval theologians were fascinated by the typological relationships through which the Old Testament was fulfilled in the New Testament. They accepted this biblical system as a kind of law of life and in this way added a layer of deeper meaning to everything they saw and read. Not only the Bible, but the lives of later saints, images in art, the acts of contemporary kings and bishops, and even the architecture of churches – all were capable of this kind of interpretation.

The Danes destroy the monastery

Sexburga died in *c.*700, and was buried near her sister Etheldreda. She was succeeded by her daughter Ermenilda, who had converted her husband Wulfhere, king of Mercia and son of the pagan Penda. After Ermenilda's death in about 700, her daughter Werburga became abbess. She however left to take charge of some Mercian nunneries. Following Etheldreda, the early abbesses all became saints. Without records we can only conjecture as to the conduct of monastic life at Ely in the eighth and early ninth centuries. In 869 the Danish Great Army arrived in East Anglia and, according to the *Anglo-Saxon Chronicle*, 'destroyed all the churches that they came to'. During this campaign, in which St Edmund was martyred, the monastic community at Ely was probably put to the sword or dispersed and the buildings burnt. After Alfred the Great had reversed the tide of Danish incursions in the 870s, he did his best to restore the beleaguered English Church, but

the idea, put forward in the *Liber Eliensis*, that he founded a college of secular clerks at Ely is open to doubt.

Could the body of Etheldreda have survived the Danish onslaught? The survival of her relics was central to the identity and prestige of the Ely community, so the author of the *Liber Eliensis*, anticipating this reasonable question, describes two episodes. In the first of these, one of the Danes, 'a satellite of the devil, breathing slaughter and blood', struck the sarcophagus with repeated sword blows until he had made an opening (still visible in the twelfth century). 'There was', we are told, 'no delay of divine vengeance, for immediately his eyes started miraculously from his head and ended there and then his sacrilegious life'. One of Alfred's seculars is recorded to have poked a stick into the crack and retrieved a piece of cloth which was quickly snatched back by the saint. He and all his family perished in consequence. These stories, devised to ward off prying eyes, were remembered with foreboding centuries later by those who moved the saint's relics for pious reasons.

4. A carved stone of c. 700 – c. 800 incorporated into one of the buildings of the hospital of St John, Ely, when it was refounded by Bishop Northwold in the thirteenth century. It is thought to show a figure blowing a horn, and a charging beast, and may have been part of the early monastery.

The power and persistence of early Christianity in the face of relentless pagan violence sprang from a new perception of life. Bede records an early convert's view of the pagan life as a sparrow emerging from the wintry night to fly briefly across a fire-lit hall only to enter the cold and dark again. The gospels, on the other hand, promised an eternal future for those who attempted to live this brief moment in a state of grace, and the Old Testament provided an account of the past that hugely extended the Saxons' idea of history. 'The people that walked in darkness have seen a great light', wrote Isaiah (9.2), 'they that dwelt in the land of the shadow of death, upon them the light hath shined.'

'Light' is one of the key words inscribed on the earliest object in the cathedral. The stone traditionally associated with Etheldreda's steward, Ovin, stands today at the west end of the south nave aisle *(Fig. 5)* and the base is inscribed, 'God give to Ovin your light and rest Amen'. It was brought to the cathedral in the eighteenth century from the nearby village of Haddenham. Ovin was a common Saxon name and modern scholarship dates the style of the inscription later than the time of Etheldreda's steward.

THE REVIVAL OF MONASTIC LIFE BY ÆTHELWOLD AND DUNSTAN

The great revival at Ely took place in the tenth century when Dunstan, archbishop of Canterbury, and Æthelwold, bishop of Winchester, reformed the English Church, under the patronage of King Edgar. The Rule of St Benedict was introduced and Byrhtnoth, prior of Winchester, was installed as abbot. Ely became one of the three centres of excellence in English monasticism as first the king, and then a sequence of other benefactors, endowed the house with the great estates that were to underpin its religious life for centuries. The key

5. *Ovin's stone. Modern scholarship suggests that it is somewhat later than the period of Etheldreda's steward of the same name. For many years it served as a mounting block in the village of Haddenham, near Ely.*

to this great renaissance was Etheldreda, and a measure of her importance in the eyes of Æthelwold is the magnificent image of her in the great book of episcopal benedictions that he commissioned for Winchester *(Col. pl. 1)*.

No one now presumed to open Etheldreda's coffin, while the church was rebuilt around her by Byrhtnoth, as described in the *Liber Eliensis*:

> those parts of it which were so much decayed by time as to have fallen down he rebuilt; and by constant application and much labour and expense, he finished all the stonework, in less time than could have been expected; and afterwards completing the roof, which had been quite destroyed by the fire; the church was so thoroughly repaired in all parts that it appeared on the whole more splendid than when it was first built.

The east end of this church was dedicated to St Peter by Archbishop Dunstan and the south side to the Blessed Virgin Mary. The monastery was also rebuilt. In the summer of 974, the body of Etheldreda's youngest sister, Withburga, was rather discreditably snatched from its shrine at West Dereham and brought to Ely by boat to lie with her family. The monks of Dereham, whose house had been founded by Withburga in 743, were subordinate to Ely. They had been temporarily befuddled by a lavish feast put on by Byrhtnoth, and could only run helplessly along the riverbank as their saint was borne swiftly away.

The Saxon church and its furnishings

We are able to visualise something of the monastery's wealth and beauty at this time from descriptive passages in the *Liber Eliensis*. One of the monks, Leo, was appointed as sub-prior to supervise the convent's increasingly complex land holdings. He had considerable skills in forestry and horticulture, planting gardens and orchards around the church and usefully opening up areas where the woodland had encroached. The beginning of an astonishing treasury of liturgical art can be traced back to this time. Leo himself donated a silver crucifix that contained some relics of St Vedast and St Amand. King Edgar had given for the altar of Etheldreda an even more magnificent gold crucifix, which also contained relics, as well as a richly decorated gospel book. Abbot Byrhtnoth installed around the high altar four large figures of the local saints, made of wood covered with silver and decorated with gold and precious stones. Needlework was the skill for which the Anglo-Saxons were famed throughout Europe. Æthelwold gave several rich copes, including a special one which had a deep gold fringe for the precentor to wear on great occasions, and Edgar gave his own robe of 'purpura' embroidered with gold. 'Purpura', a term frequently used in the description of rich Anglo-Saxon vestments, does not mean 'purple' but has been interpreted to denote a shot-silk in which a lighter colour, probably gold, glimmers through a darker one. Gold, silver, jewels, embroidered silk and the leaf gold of illuminated manuscripts reflected light. Certain jewels indeed were believed in those days to emanate a supernatural radiance.

In the gloomy and mysterious churches of the Anglo-Saxons these were visible emanations of the light invoked in the inscription on Ovin's stone and in the prophecy of Isaiah.

Six years after Edgar's death in 975 Abbot Byrhtnoth was murdered by the servants of the queen dowager, Ælfthryth, who was later to found a convent in expiation for the act. Ely also benefited from acts of repentance. For example, a certain Leofwine who confessed the murder of his mother to the pope was instructed to settle his eldest son in a monastery and endow it generously. Æthelmaer duly arrived at Ely, accompanied by the gift of significant estates. His father enlarged the church on the south side. In one porticus (one of the individual rooms often attached to the main body of a Saxon church), he built an altar to the Blessed Virgin Mary. It had an image of the Virgin enthroned – 'as tall as a man' – with the Christ Child in her lap, in silver studded with gems.

The great warrior, Byrhtnoth (not to be confused with the abbot) was entertained with his entire army at Ely in the year 991 when *en route*, as it turned out, to the celebrated Battle of Maldon. He had been turned away from Ramsey abbey, which could not cope with so great a number of guests. After his famously heroic death at the hands of the Danes, the monks brought his headless body back to Ely for burial. They completed it with a ball of wax so that he could rise entire on Judgement Day. Byrhtnoth, who had been received into the monastery before the fatal battle, had bequeathed estates to the monks. His widow Ælfflæd gave more. She also presented to the church a gold chain and an embroidered hanging depicting her husband's earlier exploits. This important Anglo-Saxon forerunner of the Bayeux Tapestry was an early example of the celebration of martial valour in a church interior.

Fear of apocalyptic destruction was part of the medieval mind but the suggestion that it was widely anticipated at the millennium is now questioned. Further Danish onslaughts followed the great defeat at the Battle of Maldon, and even after the year 1000 had passed this violence and chaos generated fear and foreboding. In 1014 Wulfstan, archbishop of York, delivered a famous homily to the English people. It began:

> Beloved men, recognise what the truth is: this world is in haste and is drawing near the end, and therefore the longer it is the worse it will get in the world. And it needs must thus become very much worse as a result of the people's sins prior to the advent of the Antichrist; and then indeed it will be terrible and cruel throughout the world.

It is a measure of the reputation of Etheldreda that Wulfstan, who died in 1023, had chosen to be buried at Ely, where he may once have been a monk *(Fig. 6)*. Ely had been seen into the second millennium by Abbot Ælfsige who, with the king's permission, had added another important relic to the church, the body of St Wendreda from March – for which he commissioned a lavish shrine. But it was carried into battle by the monks on behalf of Edmund

Ironside at Ashingdon in 1016 and captured by Cnut. Cnut was the Danish king who would soon rule over England, Denmark and Norway. His subsequent visits to Ely by boat and over the ice of Soham Mere are related in picturesque detail. His death in 1035 created a problem of succession. This led to a gruesome incident in 1036, which sheds some light on the architecture of the church at Ely. Alfred the ætheling, son of King Ethelred, was regarded as a contender for the throne by the supporters of Harold Harefoot. They blinded him before delivering him into the hands of the Ely monks. 'Nor was a more bloody deed done in this land after the Danes came, and peace made here', wrote the despairing author of the *Anglo-Saxon Chronicle*, who also added that the prince 'was worthily buried as was well fitting – as he was worthy – at the west end, near the tower in the south porticus'. This sad story demonstrates that perhaps the Anglo-Saxon church had a single west tower and that this tower was flanked by a porticus on either side. It may well have influenced the design of the present west front in the following century.

The Saxon church appears to have been

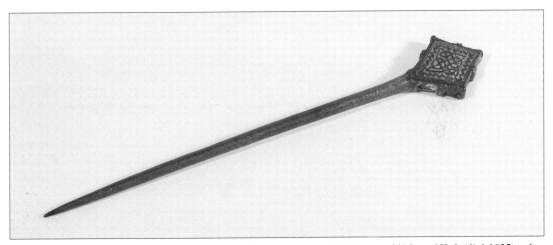

6. *Gilded bronze pin 13.2 centimetres long found at Ely in the tomb of Wulfstan, archbishop of York (died 1023), when his remains and those of six other Saxon benefactors were removed from the north side of the octagon in 1751. When Wulfstan's remains were first translated around 1154, his vestments were found to be intact and affixed with two 'gold pins', of which this is evidently one. (The Society of Antiquaries of London)*

7. *Barnack church, Northamptonshire. This tower, possibly of the late tenth century, stands near the quarry where most of the stone for Ely cathedral was extracted. (The distinctive octagonal top is of the early thirteenth century.) Similar details and techniques were probably used by the masons of Anglo-Saxon Ely.*

completely destroyed when the Normans constructed the present cathedral after 1081. Even its location is by no means certain. There can be no doubt, however, that part of it lies under the present cathedral. In 1102 the builders of the Norman church were to find it necessary to move the bodies of Ermenilda and Withburga into another part of the Saxon church because they were in the way of the advancing new building. It was not necessary, however, to move the other two saints. According to the *Liber Eliensis*:

> In the tower, to be sure, Etheldreda, Queen and famous virgin, was resplendent, entombed on the south side at her own altar, and her glorious sister, Sexburga, shone forth, buried to the north in the same place. These two olive trees of celestial mercy remained … these two columns of the house of God.

It is difficult to interpret this description of what was presumably the east end of the Saxon church. The word 'tower' may describe a kind of eastern massif incorporating tower, flanking porticus and an apse, as in the late tenth-century church at Deerhurst in Gloucestershire. The floor of the east end may have been raised up; Withburga's sarcophagus was broken by the Normans while being carried, presumably westward, down a flight of steps.

By the time this happened the Norman builders had probably reached the easternmost bays of the present nave. Recent excavations at the west end of the nave moreover revealed a small part of a substantial structure, running north under the present south-west transept. It is possible therefore (but by no means certain) that the Saxon church occupied much of the present nave with an overall length of around 60 metres, and that it had an axial tower at either end, like those of the lost tenth-century church at Ramsey. The excavation of the tenth-century church at Glastonbury founded by Dunstan has indicated a slightly larger structure. The Old

Minster at Winchester founded by Æthelwold had by 1000 reached a length of about 75 metres. Nothing is known of the architectural treatment of the Saxon church at Ely, but it would almost certainly have been built of stone from Barnack near Peterborough, where there had been a major quarry since Roman times. Barnack church has a splendid Saxon tower *(Fig. 7)* which may be as old as the late tenth century and probably gives a good idea of the techniques and designs which the Ely masons would have used at this time. Faced mainly with rubble, it is decorated in a slightly haphazard fashion with narrow bands of smooth ashlar, redolent of timber construction. Ornate sculptured panels are set into the surface, as a child might decorate a sandcastle with sea shells, and the variously shaped windows and doors are placed without any great sense of rhythm or symmetry. Internally the tower has a massive, round arch opening into the nave with elephantine moulded details distantly related to Roman buildings.

Edward the Confessor, who came to the throne in 1042, had received his early education at Ely where, we are told, he enjoyed singing godly hymns and psalms with the other boys in the cloister. He was brought to the church as a baby by his parents, King Ethelred and Queen Emma, who offered him on the high altar in a precious cloth, spotted with circular amulets and partly green in colour. (Some years later, as the queen of Cnut, Emma gave a series of wonderful textiles to the church.) Edward the Confessor was childless. By naming his cousin William of Normandy as his heir in 1051 he deliberately frustrated the interests of the powerful Earl Godwin who, he believed, had organised the murder of his brother, Alfred the ætheling.

8. The capitals of the tower arch at Barnack show the primitive but impressive character of Anglo-Saxon masonry.

Abbot Wulfric, who had taken over at Ely in 1044, died on the eve of the Norman Conquest. For a brief period the monastery was taken into the hands of Stigand, the archbishop of Canterbury, who made the last contribution to the magnificent interior of the pre-Conquest church by presenting, among other things, a great silver crucifix with a life-size image of Christ, accompanied by figures of the Virgin and St John in brass. The tenth-century reforms of Æthelwold and Dunstan had set Ely on course to become, with Winchester and Glastonbury, one of the three richest abbeys of Saxon England.

2. REBUILDING FROM THE FOUNDATIONS:
The Norman Church

The Isle of Ely is surrendered to the Normans, who reorganise the monastery. Abbot Simeon begins a new church in 1081 and in 1106 it is sufficiently advanced for his successor, Abbot Richard, to translate the relics into its eastern portion.

In 1072 William the Conqueror came to pay his respects at the shrine of Etheldreda. He would gladly have done so earlier. The Isle of Ely however, set amid treacherous and largely impassable fen, had become the last refuge of Saxon resistance. It was considered one of the best-defended places in England throughout the Middle Ages, and at the first attempt to take the isle, in 1069, the Normans had failed to make any significant headway. Trouble in the north called them away, and in the spring of 1070 their second offensive saw serious losses of men and equipment to the guerrilla campaign of Hereward the Wake. By 1071, however, the writing was on the wall. The monks, whose great estates were already being plundered by the Normans, had no alternative but to surrender the Isle of Ely. Two castles were built to secure the conquest. One guarded an entrance to the isle at Aldreth and the other, at Ely, impinged on the monastic precinct. This is likely to be the powerful earthwork now known as Cherry Hill which is still recognisable as a Norman motte-and-bailey castle. There is also later documentary evidence of another fortification at the river.

The new king removed Thurstan, who had ruled the abbey since 1066, and put it in the hands of Theodwine, a monk from the Benedictine abbey of Jumièges in Normandy. William had deprived Ely of its lands and liberties, and removed from the church all the magnificent liturgical objects which had been amassed since Æthelwold's foundation. Such acts, repeated all over England, dispersed for ever most of the greatest works of Anglo-Saxon metalwork and embroidery. But Ely was fortunate in its new abbot. He would not take office until the lands and treasures of the church had been returned. Many objects came back from the king's treasury. Theodwine died in 1075 and, after a vacancy of six years in which the abbey was administered on behalf of the king by Godfrey (another monk from Jumièges), a new abbot was appointed.

ABBOT SIMEON AND THE BUILDING OF THE NEW CHURCH

At the age of 87 Simeon can hardly have welcomed a new and demanding job but in 1081 he left his post as prior of Winchester and set out for Ely. No sooner had he taken his new office, the twelfth-century chronicler informs us, than he devoted all his energies to the construction of a new church from the foundations. He was well qualified to do so, having begun a new cathedral at Winchester with his brother, Bishop Walkelin, in 1079.

The motive for the Norman rebuilding of Ely is made explicit in the *Liber Eliensis*; it was so that the outward form might be a testament to the inner change. In Simeon's time there was a renaissance in the life of the monastery. The reorganisation of the English Church was one of the most conspicuous achievements of the Norman Conquest. Under Archbishop Lanfranc, Norman clergy took over nearly every significant position and the English monasteries were reformed along Norman lines. At Ely there was to be a new community of seventy monks and a new church whose scale and detail would be strikingly different from that of its predecessor. The great churches of the eleventh century are sometimes interpreted as a response to the first millennium. The horrors predicted by Wulfstan failed to materialise and others took a more positive view of this significant anniversary. In the words of the French monk Raoul Glaber, 'It was as though the very world had shaken herself and cast off her old age, and were clothing herself everywhere in a white robe of churches.'

The origins of the Ely plan

Where did the ideas for the Ely plan come from? The short answer is Winchester. There the great church had been building for little more than two seasons before Simeon's abrupt departure, but he must have witnessed the establishment of

THE PLAN AND USES OF THE NORMAN CHURCH

Benedictine abbeys were built so that the monks could attend to the Opus Dei, *the seven religious offices that regulated their lives. The cult of saints required room for shrines, and when monasteries were built in towns there was a demand for parish worship. These functions had to be segregated if the monks were to worship in peace. The building had also to read as a coherent whole if it was to convey an idea of the Heavenly Jerusalem (see p. 47). On certain feast days, moreover, the monks made use of the entire building for processions. Nearly all large churches were laid out in the form of a cross to signify the redemption of mankind by the Crucifixion, but this shape was partitioned at ground level by substantial screens in stone or timber. It was only above these screens that the majestic, overarching unity of the building was apparent.*

At this period shrines were placed at the east end, behind the high altar. The monks sang their services in a choir immediately to the west. At Ely their choir would occupy the central volume of the east arm and extend through the crossing into the second bay of the nave. The crossing tower therefore stood above the choir and its bells signified to the outside world the devotions of the monks. Major churches had an additional tower (often a pair) at the west end, and the bells here were rung at major feasts and on other special occasions. The central volume of the nave would be given over to the parish and this area would be divided from the monks' choir by a stone screen or pulpitum (see p. 35).

the plan and the foundations. If the Norman plans of Winchester and Ely are compared *(Figs. 9 and 10)*, the similarities are immediately apparent. The whole east arm and crossing of

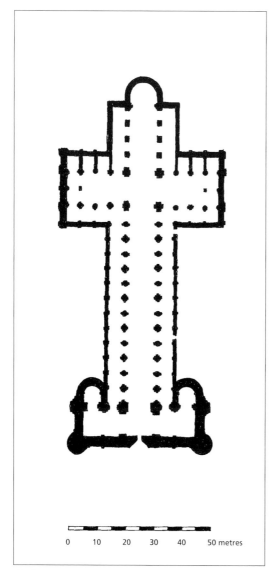

9. A reconstruction of the ground plan of Norman Ely (1081–1140). (After Eric Fernie)

10. The plan of Walkelin's cathedral at Winchester (begun 1079). (After Eric Fernie)

Norman Ely now lies under the present thirteenth- and fourteenth-century choir and octagon, so this part of the plan is a reconstruction by Eric Fernie, based on archaeological evidence. It was simpler than that of Winchester, where a crypt and curving ambulatory corridor formed the plan of the upper church. The forerunner of this part of Ely is possibly the three-apse choir of St Ouen at Rouen, the church

where Simeon was a monk before the Conquest. The nave at Ely was a mighty thirteen bays long. It ended in a western block composed of a pair of transepts with turrets, and eastern apsidal chapels. This remarkable composition was quite unlike Winchester. Apart from these differences at the extremities, the plan of Winchester was clearly the starting point for Ely. The immense scale distinguishes these two churches from anything in Normandy or England up to this date. The other exceptional feature is the luxurious use in the transepts of aisles on both sides, like those of the nave and choir.

The side aisles had two functions. Those on the east of the main transepts housed chapels but the others throughout the church were for processions. It was not intended that people should pass through individual openings in the arcades except at designated places. Ely displays in the main transepts and in part of the nave what appear to be remains of a continuous stone plinth or stylobate. This step, on which the piers stand, can also be seen in John Crook's reconstruction of the choir at Winchester. It would have controlled movement around the church.

Roman planning principles

The plans of many Romanesque buildings can be related to ancient traditions of church design. In a striking diagram, Fernie has super-imposed the Ely plan onto that of the early Christian basilica of S. Paolo-fuori-le-Mura in Rome *(Fig. 11)*. This shows that the proportions governing the layout of the basilica are the same as those of Ely. The conqueror's own church at Caen can be fitted into the same scheme but is much shorter than Ely. The term 'Romanesque' is used to describe the architecture of the late eleventh and twelfth century because the forms and details are consciously derived from Roman buildings. Fernie's diagram shows how the designer of Ely was imbued with Roman prin-ciples of scale and planning. Even though Anglo-Norman builders might not have the need for five-aisled Roman naves like that of S. Paolo, they could none the less obtain comparable grand measurements in length. In the case of Ely this meant an internal dimension of 387 feet [118 m]. How does this compare with the other great churches of the Conquest? Winchester's internal length was 515 feet

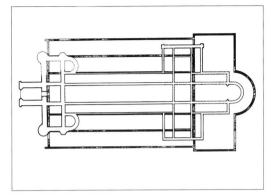

11. Diagram of the plan of Norman Ely superimposed on that of S. Paolo-fuori-le-Mura, Rome (begun 385). (Eric Fernie)

[157 m], Norwich Cathedral was 433 feet 132 m] and the abbey of Bury St Edmunds was 485 feet [148 m].

Laying out the church

It would take nearly sixty years to complete most of Norman Ely so it was necessary to construct the building in usable sections. The east end, comprising the east arm, the crossing, the transepts and two bays of the nave, was the most urgent. This proved to be a 25-year campaign, so for religious life to continue, the great build-ing site could not compromise the Saxon church and monastery.

Although Simeon had extensive experience of building, it is unlikely that he would have designed the new church. This job would have been given to a master mason. In the later Middle Ages the mason would have laid out the plan on vellum, or on a plastered wall or floor (see p. **57**), using a pair of compasses and an L-shaped square. A number of sweeping and intersecting arcs would begin to determine key points, and in this way a system of geometrically derived proportions would be established for all elements of the plan. No design drawings for Anglo-Norman buildings exist but the business of laying out a church is thought to have been identical to the drawing process just described. The first step at Ely was to clear a great area of ground, probably to the east of the Saxon church, so that the east end and transepts could be set out. A rope tied to a stake would take the place of the compasses and, under the master's direction, the workforce would rapidly determine the critical points. A unit of measurement was multiplied to fix all the dimensions. Eric Fernie has established that at Ely this unit was 5 feet 6 inches [1.67 m], and that the multiples that fix the main dimensions are in a strict proportional system which might, at first, appear arbitrary. They were generated from the relationship between the sides of a square and its diagonal which, as Pythagoras demonstrated, is 1 to the square root of 2. The distance from the aisle wall to the central axis is 7 units. From the aisle wall to the opposite arcade is 10 units and to the opposite wall is 14. These almost magically harmonious proportions, which underlie the whole plan, could be easily generated with ropes and stakes. They were used throughout the Middle Ages for all aspects of architectural design and they explain the orderly beauty of much medieval work.

Materials and techniques of construction

Trenches were then dug and the foundations laid in them. The Norman foundations of the south transept, laid bare in the nineteenth century and recorded by John Bacon, the clerk of works, were according to his reckoning 5 feet 8 inches [1.73 m] deep. This suggests 1 unit. The base was the thin outcrop of greensand, a soft, brownish stone which overlies the clay that raises the Isle of Ely above the surrounding fen. On this the masons placed a thin layer of rammed greensand lumps interspersed with clunch (a local soft chalk). Next came a thin layer of small greensand stones. None of this was bound with mortar but above it was 4 feet [1.22 m] of rubble stone laid in a mortar of lime

and rough sand. On this surface the walls of the church were raised. Their thickness matched the depth of the foundations.

The facing stones of Norman Ely came from Barnack, near Peterborough, and were brought by river, down the Nene to the Wash and then up the Great Ouse. Transport by water was considerably easier and cheaper than by road, so the considerable distance from the quarry to the new building was not a great problem.

One of the main differences between Saxon and post-Conquest buildings was the much greater quantities of good-quality ashlar facing stone used by the Normans. The walling of the Norman work at Ely is completely clad with ashlar both inside and out. This is a formidable structural skin; but the core of each wall, including the great piers and arches of the interior, consists of greensand rubble *(Fig. 23)*. Greensand also provides the aggregate for the lime mortar in which the individual stones are bedded, and it actually appears as a surface walling material in some of the early monastic buildings at Ely. Much of the Norman stone would have been worked on the site, but it is probable that quantities were dressed at the quarry to save weight in transport. Individual Norman stones can be recognised today, even

12. (right) The north transept. Although they began in 1081, it would be half a century before the Norman builders reached the west front. During much of this period the handsomely detailed north transept façade was the face that the new abbey church showed to the town. Conical stone roofs were added to the turrets in the mid-thirteenth century. The gable was altered to match the unusual four-sided shape of a 1330s roof which was itself replaced c.1470. The tall Perpendicular windows are early fifteenth century. In 1699 the whole of the right-hand side collapsed and was swiftly rebuilt in replica. Only the rusticated doorway and the window above were built in a contemporary idiom. To the left is the façade of the Lady chapel (1321–53). (Photograph by Philip Dixon)

when they are reused in later work, by the rough striated tooling: diagonal for blocks and vertical for cylinders and rolls.

As the building rose, so would the network of timber scaffold poles bound together with ropes and fixed to the building in put-log holes. These holes were usually closed by a single facing stone, or patch of render, when the scaffolding was removed. The vertical distance between them represents the maximum height to which a mason could comfortably lay stone. The soft mortar has relatively weak adhesive properties and serves merely to cushion stones which are held together by gravity. Wedge-shaped voussoirs, which compose the great arches, would be arranged on elaborate timber centring

or 'falsework'. A much more complex centring of timber was needed for the construction of the aisle vaults. These groin vaults *(Fig. 13)*, whose shape corresponds to the intersection of two half-cylinders, needed a huge wooden mould on which the masons could lay flat stones, bedded in thick mortar on edge. Once the mass of the vault was complete, the timber-work was removed and the underside coated in a layer of render. A similar technique was used to create the semi-cylindrical vaults of wall passages and spiral staircases. In some of these the final coat of render has fallen away to reveal the imprint of innumerable centring planks *(Fig. 14)*. Sometimes the wooden centring itself still clings to the underside.

13. The heavy groin vaults of the south nave aisle are divided into bays by transverse arches of dressed stone. The subtle change in their profile signifies a new building phase.

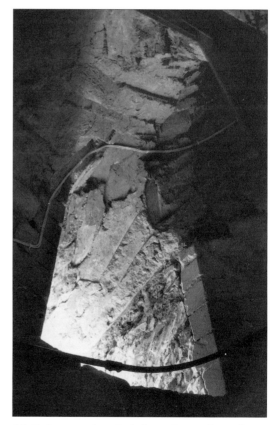

14. Staircase vault and window embrasure in south-west transept. A ramshackle arrangement of twelfth-century shuttering planks has left clear impressions on the render.

15. Winchester cathedral, south transept. Walkelin's transepts may have been complete by 1093. They closely resemble the work of his brother Simeon at Ely. (National Monuments Record)

The elevation design: the main transepts

The building of Norman Winchester proceeded apace. Its choir was ready for use by 1093, whereas Ely's was consecrated in 1106. In both cases the original choirs were later rebuilt, so the earliest complete Norman architecture of both churches is in the transepts *(Col. pl. 2 and Figs. 1 and 15)*. The elevations are closely comparable in appearance and derive from a scheme which survives at an early date in the church of St Remi at Rheims (1005–49). The great walls are organised in uniform bays and in three generous storeys. The second storey, the tribune (sometimes called the triforium), is very nearly as tall as the ground-floor arcade and is subdivided by a delicate central column. The top storey, or clerestory, whose purpose is to admit direct light to the central vessel, is somewhat less tall and has a continuous wall passage. This passage is possible because of the great thickness of the wall. The technique of thick-wall construction is a Norman speciality. It was so widely deployed in England that the tradition persisted into the fourteenth century and beyond, especially where, as at Ely, the masons were extending or converting Norman work.

The interiors of Norman Ely and Winchester were surmounted by the great horizontal tie beams of an open timber roof. A visual reminder of this arrangement survives at Ely in the powerful horizontal moulding on the west wall of the nave, and Gavin Simpson has reconstructed the carpentry of the Norman roof *(Fig. 20)*. Early Christian basilicas in Rome had similar plain timber roofs, and just as the plan communicates something of their layout and scale, so the elevation of Ely, with its solemn repetition of round arches, speaks the language of great Roman structures like the Colosseum in Rome and the Aula Regia at Trier. For the medieval Church, as the heir of the Roman Empire, such ancient buildings were the epitome of monumental architecture. Their grandeur and authority were to be harnessed for the glory of God, whatever their original purpose.

The lost Norman choirs of Ely and Winchester

Interesting though it is to compare the transepts of Winchester and Ely, it would be even more helpful if we could examine the elevations of the vanished eastern limbs. These would normally have been the earliest part of the building to be completed. What survives of the old choir at Ely after its rebuilding in later centuries is not very extensive but quite revealing. At the east end the central space terminated in a full-height apse, as at Peterborough. The wall shafts by which this apse was framed still survive: a sliver of masonry between the present thirteenth- and fourteenth-century

16. (left) The nave of the abbey church of Jumièges, Normandy (1046–66). The big double bays and alternating supports were much emulated in England, first in Edward the Confessor's church at Westminster, begun c.1050 (demolished in the thirteenth century), and then at Winchester and Ely. (Conway Library, Courtauld Institute of Art)

17. (above) The birds and beasts carved on the capitals of the south transept are among the earliest Norman sculptures in England. They closely resemble the border decorations of the Bayeux Tapestry (1066–82).

choir bays. It is only because these later choirs seem to have adopted the former, Norman levels that we can comment on the early elevation design. It was the same overall height as the transepts and was arranged in the same three-storey pattern with arcade, tribune and clerestory. The measurements differ from the transept elevations in one respect: the tribune floor is 40 inches [1 m] higher, a small but significant detail.

John Crook's reconstruction of the lost choir of Winchester reveals a corresponding but even greater discrepancy in the height of the tribune floor, and there it was caused arguably by the crypt on which the choir was built. There was no crypt at Ely and yet this quirk of the Winchester design appears to have been transferred, perhaps to add distinction to the choir.

PROBLEMS WITH PIERS

At Winchester, the alternation of the piers between drum and compound shapes was the special ornament of the choir. At Ely it was to be used for the whole church. This extended use of alternation was a feature of some of the earliest Romanesque buildings and, although not common in Normandy, was used at Jumièges, the monastery which provided Ely with two successive Norman leaders after the Conquest.

If we examine the elevation of Jumièges (Fig. 16), we can see how the alternation is used to create a system of great double bays which are framed by thin shafts rising the full height of the wall from each compound pier. In this system the slighter cylindrical piers are related to their ultimate Roman forerunners in having deep capitals which, according to the rules of the Corinthian order, should correspond to the column diameter. The columns at Jumièges are, however, much stockier in proportion than would have been allowed in a Roman building. By the time of the Conquest, moreover, the Normans had begun to build with thicker walls. Whatever advantages this conferred on the upper elevation (stability and access passages), at the ground floor it simply meant fatter piers. The Corinthian column which, according to the Roman architect Vitruvius, imitated 'the slenderness of a maiden' becomes at Ely a truly formidable matron. It is a good example of how the practical outcome of a building method could force the medieval designer out of the classical tradition into another form.

Shafts could be added to the compound piers to increase their bulk without wholly abandoning the Roman principle of proportion in the capitals. But the inflation of the cylindrical piers into great drums stretched the capital horizontally so that its classical origins were almost unrecognisable. The space between the corner volutes has

to be filled with an extended pattern of interlace. It is interesting to see how the masons of the later phases at Ely wrestled with the aesthetic problems of the drum pier capitals and their relationship to the compound piers set up in this earliest work (Fig. 15).

When he built his transepts, the mason of Winchester switched from alternation to a system of uniform compound piers (Fig. 15). In so doing, he avoided a problem that was to give the builders of Ely quite a headache. At Winchester the middle, tribune storey is carried round the end of the transepts on an open bridge, which is the full width of the aisle. Ely once had these broad bridges across the ends of both transepts' arms, but before the church was finished, they were replaced by the present, narrow wall walks (see p. 29). The Winchester system guaranteed a good, strong compound pier at the point where the aisle turned the corner and sprung the arches of the bridge. At Ely the alternating supports required more careful planning if a compound pier was to appear in the right place. In the south transept at Ely (see Fig. 1), they sprung the lost bridge from the weaker drum pier. When it came to the design of the north transept (Col. pl. 2), this was clearly thought to be unsatisfactory. So the whole rhythm of the alternation was thrown out of kilter in order to get a compound pier at the corner of the lost bridge.

The loss of the four Norman crossing piers in the great collapse of 1322 makes it difficult to be certain about the inner ends of the transept arcades, but if we were to represent the rhythms of the two transepts by letters, making P the compound pier and C the columnar drum pier, then the south transept probably ran a symmetrical PCPCP, whereas the north may have run PPCPP.

ABBOT RICHARD AND THE SECOND TRANSLATION OF ETHELDREDA

In 1088 Simeon suffered a stroke. William II appointed his chaplain Ranulf Flambard to supervise the monastery during the abbot's indisposition. It is not known whether this able but self-interested administrator simply milked the abbey of its revenues or devoted some of them energetically towards the building work. Simeon's death at the age of 99 in 1093 was followed by a vacancy. A new abbot, Richard de Clare, took office in 1100. He was deposed by

18. (left and below) The design of capitals at Ely shows the Norman masons engaging with the problems of a developing architectural language. In the capital of a drum pier in the south transept (top) the volutes which looked well on the capitals of smaller shafts (e.g. Fig. 17) are now too far apart for comfort and interlacing foliage has to be stretched between them. Cushion capitals (above left) are introduced for the first time at Ely on the west side of the north transept. But this form does not look happy on the adjacent drum pier (left), whose great girth distorts the proportions. In the earliest work of the nave this effect is mediated by building great shafts against the front of each drum (bottom left) to give them something of the character of the compound piers with which they alternate. In the later phase of the nave (below) a new mason takes this a step further, expressing the angles of the tall shafts as rolls, two of which are fitted neatly under the overhanging corners of the capital.

Henry I two years later and had to go to Rome to plead his own cause, returning vindicated to Ely in 1103. Etheldreda, he believed, had helped him in his hour of need, and now he dedicated all his energies to the completion of her church. The chronicler records that at this time the growing new building had already come up against the old one.

As early as 1102 the building operations necessitated the removal of the bodies of Ermenilda and Withburga from the old building. Their shrines may have been at the extreme east end of the Saxon church. Various vertical construction breaks in the aisle walls of the nave suggest that the masons of the new work were gradually disposing of a predecessor as they worked westward. The new church, according to the *Liber Eliensis,* seemed:

> Thanks to a certain judiciousness of its architectural design and the superiority and grace of its fine-wrought craftsmanship, to be worthy to be preferred by beholders over all the churches in the same kingdom, whether constructed in past ages or built anew in our own time.

In October 1106, on the anniversary of Etheldreda's first translation Abbot Richard's building was ready to receive the relics.

> Out of deep yearning he desired and purposed within his own time to translate the body of the most holy virgin Etheldreda from the old church into the new – from a modest [church] into a greater and more beautiful one. [In this he was] mindful of the fact that Joseph translated the body of his father from the land of Egypt into the land of Canaan, so that it might receive greater reverence. [His purpose was] that so bright a lamp and shining light should not hide under a bushel but rather be set upon a lamp-stand and should become clearly visible and shine forth to the advantage of all, in the presence of witnesses, and amid the thronging multitudes.

The abbot invited many important guests and although several, including Anselm, archbishop of Canterbury, pleaded prior engagements, a good company of senior clergy attended. Bishop Herbert of Norwich preached a sermon on the life, death and miracles of Etheldreda, which moved everyone to tears. Then a strange thing is reported to have happened.

> There came about thunderings of a storm and lightning bolts of such a kind that almost all the windows of the church were broken by jagged lightning strikes, and frequent flashes fell down onto the pavement near the holy bodies. And it was a miraculous thing that the fire fell without the effect natural to it amidst wood and straw; and other flammable materials changed their quality, so that whatever of this sort fell into the church was harmless. This great miracle worked by that saintly woman happened thus, according to the opinion of some, so that she might show by means of the terror from heaven that she was displeased at being so handled in public, but she did nothing to harm the church in this indignation of hers, so that it would escape no one's notice that the stars of heaven were obedient to her behest … Archbishop Anselm … residing as he was far away in Kent, on seeing the heaven riven with such tumult, said, 'I know that our brother Richard, the Abbot of Ely, has today translated his saints and treated them irreverently, and I have no doubt that this stormy weather is a sign of bad omen.' Nor was his opinion mistaken, because few of those who were present at the time and had seen Withburga face to face survived the whole year.

Abbot Richard indeed died less than a year later, on 17 June 1107, but many of the other clergy did live out their days. Richard had taken care not to open Etheldreda's coffin but, as the author of the *Liber Eliensis* describes, there had been an accident in carrying Withburga's sarcophagus and a new one had to be made. The incorruption of Withburga *(Col. pl. 4)* had

19. The north arcade of Thorney abbey nave. The alternating supports are closely comparable to the earliest parts of the nave at Ely, and are known to have been finished before 1110. The arches were blocked after the Reformation.

The design of the nave

No one can say with certainty how much building had been achieved by this date. It seems likely that the monastic choir was complete. This would imply that the transepts were built, and that work had begun on the easternmost bays of the nave *(Col. pl. 3)*. The rival pier systems of the two transepts presented an interesting dilemma for the design of the nave.

This could have been the moment to break with the alternating system and adopt the uniform compound piers found in the Norman nave of Winchester. In the event, the nave was an ingenious compromise. It was developed from the design of the north transept which, like Jumièges, had incorporated wall shafts running the full height of the elevation from the compound piers. The nave sustained the alternating system but now combined it with a full-height shaft in *every* bay. This scheme achieves the best of both worlds. It clearly relates to the alternating supports of the transepts, but the additional wall shafts greatly enrich the long vista from the west door. The compact grouping of small and large cylinders in the arcade and tribune generates the supple linearity that makes Ely one of the best Norman naves in England. Nearly all the hard corners of the early Norman work are now softened with angle rolls. This development is first noticeable in the upper levels of the transepts but the complete effect can only be seen in the nave.

Some further reassurance that work on this magnificent elevation had been initiated very early in the twelfth century is provided by the nave of nearby Thorney abbey, where a similarly complex alternating system is used. Gunter of Le Mans, Thorney's abbot, was present at Etheldreda's eventful translation and was at that time in the process of building his church. It was completed in 1109 and the towers of the west front were finished in 1110 *(Fig 19)*.

never, it seems, been verified so this was an ideal opportunity to do so. There are graphic details of her flexible limbs and wonderful beauty. But the new coffin was mysteriously too short for the body and, in spite of numerous carefully measured adjustments, it remained so. Then it was found that the old coffin had miraculously repaired itself. Verifiable incorruption and an additional miracle are evidence of a campaign to enhance the cult of Withburga and the whole story of the translation shows how completely the Norman community had adopted the Saxon saints.

Plate 1. The Benedictional of St Æthelwold (British Library, MS Add. 49598, f. 90b). Bishop Æthelwold, who refounded Ely and Winchester as Benedictine monasteries in 970, commissioned the book from the monastic scriptorium at Winchester between 971 and 984. This exceptionally magnificent full-page miniature of St Etheldreda shows her importance in his eyes. (Reproduced by permission of the British Library)

Plate 2. (above) The interior of the north transept (1081–1106) gives the most complete impression of the early Norman design. Roll mouldings introduced in the building of the middle storey – the tribune – softened the severe angles of the early work. (Photograph by Philip Dixon)

Plate 3. (right) The nave was completed in the first quarter of the twelfth century. The painted ceiling was applied to the underside of the thirteenth-century roof in 1858–64 (see Col. pl. 15) and Gilbert Scott's fine floor was laid in 1869–70. (Photograph by Philip Dixon)

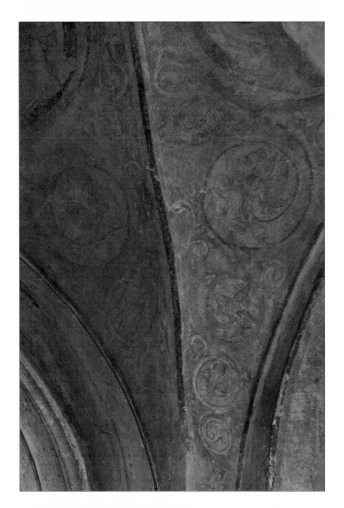

Plate 4. *Romanesque painting at Ely: (left) A vault in one of the eastern bays of the south nave aisle has the earliest wall painting in the cathedral. It is strikingly similar to the sculpted foliage of the nearby Monks' Door (Fig. 25) and to the initial letter at the beginning of a book of miracles (Cambridge, Corpus Christi College MS 393) written and illuminated at Ely some time between 1116 and 1141 (below left). An initial from the same manuscript (below right) begins the life of Withburga and encloses a rare image of the saint. In one hand she holds a lily, a symbol of her chastity (verified by Abbot Richard's public exposure of her incorrupt body in 1106) and in the other the crown that is her heavenly reward. (With permission of the Master and Fellows of Corpus Christi College, Cambridge)*

Plate 5. *(right) Bishop Northwold's presbytery (1234–52) was designed to provide a magnificent setting for the shrine of Etheldreda and to celebrate her power and prestige. It was also a monument to Northwold, whose tomb lay in the centre of the building at the feet of Etheldreda.*

Plate 6. Reconstruction by E.W. Tristram (1882–1952) of the thirteenth-century decorative painting in the cathedral: the south side of the nave. (Victoria & Albert Museum)

Plate 7. (right) The lantern interior. William Hurley, the king's carpenter, spanned the octagon with one of the most daring and innovative timber structures of the Middle Ages. The present painted decoration was undertaken by Thomas Gambier Parry in 1873 and illustrates the 150th Psalm. It effaced the remains of medieval decoration by Master Walter the painter, which included painted window tracery on the vault webs. (Photograph by Philip Dixon)

Plate 8. (above) The fragments of the Lady chapel's stained glass give a tantalising glimpse of an interior that was once saturated in rich colour and alive with imagery. (Photograph by Keith Barley)

Plate 9. (above right) Lady chapel, painted stonework. Although there is not much evidence of painted stone at the west end of the chapel, there is a good deal of vibrant colour and gold leaf in the architecture of the eastern bays.

Plate 10. (below) The important part played by the colourful vestments of the clergy in the liturgy of the medieval cathedral is shown by this fine cope of 1470–1500. The orphrey is embroidered with figures of saints and the green velvet is worked with 'waterflowers'. The monastic chronicle records the many costly vestments given to the church by its bishops. In 1169, for example, amongst those left by Bishop Nigel was an alb with wonderful beasts and birds worked in gold thread. His cope was called Gloria Mundi.

3. The Twelfth Century:
A Cathedral in the Making

In 1109 Ely is raised to cathedral status. The building of the west front, beginning in c.1130, is a long project and while it is under way changes, possibly connected with the liturgy, are made to the rest of the church. This work coincides with the troubled episcopate of Bishop Nigel. After 1174 Bishop Ridel completes the cathedral by finishing the western transepts and building the west tower. Over the century of building the cathedral displays the gradual development of Romanesque and the early impact of the new gothic style.

Abbot Richard wanted to express his new-found veneration for Withburga by making her a silver shrine. As the *Liber Eliensis* tells us, however, 'other occupations in various ways kept him back from this undertaking, and particularly the fact that he was striving to bring to nought the calumnies of the bishops of Lincoln, by changing the monastery into an episcopal see'. He had in fact followed the precedent of Simeon in accepting the benediction of the bishop of Lincoln, a gesture that infringed Ely's ancient autonomy and prestige. His successor Hervey, appointed as administrator during the vacancy following Richard's death in 1107, was the former bishop of Bangor. Having failed to subdue his rebellious Welsh diocese by force of arms, he was searching for another bishopric.

It must have seemed a great moment for Ely when in 1109 the pope agreed to create a new see out of the eastern fringe of the Norman diocese of Lincoln, but there was a price to be paid. The possessions of the great abbey, the lands and revenues, now had to be split between the bishop on the one hand and the prior and convent on the other. The abbey lost half its income and protested that it could no longer support more than forty monks. Before the Conquest Ely was one of the richest abbeys in England. Once it had become a cathedral it was still wealthy, but trailed behind Gloucester and Worcester. The bishop became titular abbot and was entitled to have his throne – the *cathedra* – at the east end of the choir (see p. **40**). Apart from this alteration in the furniture, no other measure was necessary to distinguish the building from its previous role. Years of wrangling lay ahead and the task of completing the half-built leviathan must have looked problematic.

The division of the property was a bad start for a relationship which, in the time of Bishop Hervey's colourful successor, Nigel, was to become even more disagreeable. But in another way the status of Ely was to be considerably enhanced by association with the bishops, who

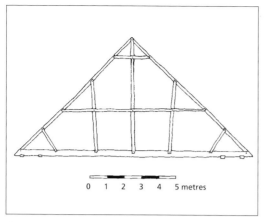

20. *The design of the Norman nave roof c.1120. (After a reconstruction by Gavin Simpson)*

were usually great statesmen, operating at the centre of things and generally far away from the Fens. They sent forth their impressed images on documents in seals of increasing grandeur and pretension *(Fig. 35)*, and in the centuries to come were to leave their imprint, positive and negative, on the architecture of the cathedral.

THE COMPLETION OF THE NAVE

How long did it take to complete the nave and when did the masons start to build the present west front? No document really helps with this question and the evidence of the architecture itself is ambiguous. Changes of detail and breaks in construction have been identified by Sarah Ferguson. Her suggestion is that the nave was completed relatively rapidly and she points to the appearance of certain details similar to those in the choir of Peterborough, tradition-ally believed to have been begun after a fire in 1117. A subsequent tree-ring analysis of one of the timbers of the nave roof at Ely (a thirteenth-century reconstruction using a lot of Norman timber) has suggested a felling date of after *c.*1120. The harmonious overall impression is certainly suggestive of swift progress.

The west front

In its complete state, the west front was one of the most magnificent of Anglo-Norman church façades. The huge bell tower grew from a pair of richly ornate transepts which projected double-storey chapels on their eastern flanks and sported four bold corner turrets with complex plans *(Fig. 22)*. The alteration of the west tower in the fourteenth century and the loss of the northern arm, probably in the fifteenth century, have significantly changed the ensemble.

It is to the Rhineland rather than Normandy

BISHOP NIGEL

Nigel, who took office in 1133, was the treasurer of Henry I but the king's death in 1135 opened the civil war between Stephen and Henry's daughter and chosen heir, the Empress Matilda. Ely was once more embattled as Nigel, who supported Matilda, fortified the isle, strengthening its castles. Stephen captured Ely in 1139/40 but Nigel's followers had recovered themselves by 1142, which prompted another armed occupation – by Geoffrey de Mandeville – in that year. The war ended in 1148 and in 1154, on the accession of Henry II, Nigel became treasurer again. During this long period Nigel's desperate need for money had been met by raiding funds which the monks regarded as their own. He had seized and pawned some of the great treasures of the church and the silver had even been stripped from one side of Etheldreda's shrine. But as early as 1144/5 he had granted to the monks the manor of Hadstock to make good some of these losses. The monks' interpretation was that it was to be used more generally for the building of the church (operationes ecclesie), which could be taken to suggest that some work was in process or in prospect at this time.

21. The south-west transept interior (lower part c.1130) is one of the most ornate of English Romanesque interiors. Used for many years after the Reformation as a workshop, its arcaded walls were carefully restored by Willis in 1844, when partitions were removed to reunite it with the western crossing. (National Monuments Record)

that we must look for surviving comparisons with this kind of western complex. In the great churches of that region the western block is often composed around an axial bell tower. The tradition, which begins in the tenth century, produces recognisable forerunners for Ely in St Pantaleon at Cologne (960–80) and St Michael at Hildesheim (1010–33). It appears in developed Romanesque form in the abbey church of Maria Laach (1093–1156), which has the ship-like massing of Ely. If the cathedral were tapping into a Rhenish tradition at this date, it may also have reflected the form of pre-Conquest Ely (see p. **9**). The lateral spread of the Ely transepts

is more pronounced than most of the German examples and this is a general tendency in English west fronts, illustrated in the contemporary western block at Bury St Edmunds, where one of the upper chapels was dedicated in 1142.

The quality of the detail is in some ways inferior to that of the nave but the decoration is in every way richer. The west front was often a place for the display of rich ornament, but usually this is confined to the exterior *(Fig. 29)*. The remarkable thing about the Ely work is the density of ornament on its inner walls *(Fig. 21)*. It is almost as though we were stepping into a different church and it is quite conceivable that

27

these architectural fireworks were intended to underline the significance of a new liturgical focus at the west end.

The west front was built slowly and in stages *(Col. pl. 18)*. There are three basic design phases. Phase 1 took the work to tribune floor level. Phase 2 was interrupted but completed most of the tribune storey. In a completely distinct third phase, whose details are gothic, the masons completed some of the details of the tribune, built the whole of the clerestories and constructed the west tower (see p. **37**). A detailed archaeological study by Kate Fearn and Pamela Marshall has used masons' marks and an analysis of mortar joints to show the individual campaigns in which the south-west transept was constructed.

Transept bridges and cloister doors

There are several indications that during the construction of the west front the masons, who were still building the nave clerestory, went back over the church and made a few changes and enrichments. Firstly, there is the surprising alteration to the gallery bridges of the main transepts. The interlacing arcades of the altered south transept bridge *(Fig. 26)* are of the same type as those found on the interior walls of the south-west transept *(Fig. 21)*. This would suggest that the bridges were altered after the completion of the main body of the nave when work was under way on the front.

During the campaign in which the bridges were altered, a wall (now much restored) decorated with similar interlacing arches was

23. *The remains of the north-west transept still clinging to the western crossing. The rubble core of the Norman wall is clearly exposed on the left of the photograph. The architectural detail is in some places earlier than the south side. Also visible is one of the great inner reinforcing arches introduced into the crossing in 1405–7. It may have pre-dated the great collapse, but the large raking buttress was possibly built in c.1474–5 to support the tower after the loss of the transept.*

22. *(left) The western tower and south-west transept seen from the south transept roof. They were begun c.1130 and almost completed by Bishop Ridel (1174–89). The octagonal top of the tower is late fourteenth century and the large apsidal chapel (now dedicated to St Catharine) was reconstructed by Robert Willis in 1849. (National Monuments Record)*

inserted between the columns on the west side of the south transept, to create a vestry. This aisle once had its own entrance from the cloister. During much of the early Norman building campaign this entrance had probably been the principal door to the church from the monastery. In the phase of work under consideration this doorway was diminished by the introduction of a lower arch, beautifully decorated with carved foliage *(Fig. 25)*.

24. (left) The Prior's Door (c.1120–40) has a magnificent carved tympanum of Christ in Judgement (above) and its jambs are decorated with the signs of the zodiac. Christian artists used the pagan calendar to express the yearly round of devotion and work. The tympanum, on the other hand, reminded the monks that all time ended in judgement: 'and behold there was a door opened in heaven, and the first voice which I heard, a voice as of a trumpet speaking with me, one saying come up hither, and I will show thee the things which must come to pass hereafter … and behold there was a throne set in heaven; and one sitting upon the throne; And he that sat was to look upon like a jasper stone and a sardius: and there was a rainbow round about the throne' (Revelation 4.1–3).

George Zarnecki has established that this decorated inner arch belongs with the two other wonderful doorways that open into the cloister: the Monks' Door and the Prior's Door. These doorways, whose names are a relatively recent invention, may have been introduced *after* the nave south aisle was completed. The Prior's Door in particular registers unhappily with the adjacent wall arcades. The entrance into the south transept aisle was reduced to a scale appropriate to its new role as a vestry door and thus gave greater emphasis to the new Monks' Door, which stood next to it at right angles. The Monks' Door now became the main entrance from the cloister to the monks' choir which, it will be remembered,

stretched into the two eastern bays of the nave. The sculptural style of these doorways has been compared by Zarnecki with decorated initials in a book of miracles written and illuminated in the Ely scriptorium during the first half of the twelfth century *(Col. pl. 4, bottom)*. He dates the doorways to *c.*1135 but some would see them as part of the original nave build (completed *c.*1120) while others would date them even later than 1135. What is incontestable, however, is the unity of style in the Romanesque art at Ely. The foliage forms in sculpture and manuscript illumination are also to be seen in the only really impressive piece of Norman wall painting that survives in the cathedral.

25. The Monks' Door c.1120–40 (to the left) was the means by which the monks entered their choir. Its cusps are decorated with figures of kneeling priors holding pastoral staffs. It replaced an earlier entrance (to the right) in which a lower decorative arch was inserted when it was reduced in status to a vestry door. The great buttress that overlaps both doorways was introduced in 1322–8 to support the octagon.

26. The decorative walkway across the end of the south transept was built when a much deeper bridge was demolished. The similarly decorated but much restored vestry wall was built at the same time. Both resemble the arcading in the south-west transept (Fig. 21).

Romanesque wall painting

Little is known about the earliest decoration of the Norman church. At other early Norman cathedrals the walls were covered with a fictive masonry pattern of red lines on white. Individual chapels and important sites would certainly have been painted with images. In the south aisle of the nave at Ely *(Col. pl. 4, top)*, on one of the vaults, there are the remains of a splendid scheme in which roundels with indistinct figure subjects are set in a field of excellent foliage patterns. It spans the site of a chapel called in the late thirteenth-century sacrist's accounts *Crux ad Fontem* (the Cross at the Spring) (see p. **82**) and may therefore celebrate the site of Etheldreda's first burial. Here, after her translation by Sexburga, a miraculous spring

welled forth which in the Norman church fed a cistern whose healing properties were recorded in the *Liber Eliensis*. The cloister doorways also have traces of paint, which suggest that their foliage was picked out in similar colours.

The translation of the seven Saxon benefactors

The remains of the benefactors are now contained in seven little boxes built into the wall of Bishop West's chapel, but they have only been there since the eighteenth century. From the twelfth century they were buried on the north side of the church (in the fourteenth century this certainly meant on the north side of the main crossing, behind the stalls of the monks) (see p. **65**). The benefactors, who included the warrior, Byrhtnoth, and Wulfstan, archbishop of York, are written about at length in the *Liber Eliensis*. They had been removed (at an unknown date) from their first resting place in the Saxon building in order to allow the construction of the Norman church. They were then given a temporary burial deep in the monks' cemetery next to the chancel (i.e. the east end). There they remained until, many years later 'in Prior Alexander's time, late in the reign of King Stephen', they were exhumed, with some difficulty, and solemnly interred again 'in the north part of the church'. The date of this translation is likely to have been around 1154 and it seems possible that, as with the translation of Etheldreda in 1106, this prestigious reinterment marked some notable stage in the construction process. The completion of some of the works just discussed is one possibility. But what was the motive for these alterations and for the lavish character of the new work to the west?

Liturgical traditions

The Rule of St Benedict specified the order of services and gave an indication of their content but in the course of time individual communities developed local traditions. If the Benedictine movement were to remain vital it needed periodic reform. When Ely was re-founded by Æthelwold in 970, he introduced a new set of rules that applied to all English Benedictines, called the *Regularis Concordia*. This held sway generally until the Norman Conquest, when Archbishop Lanfranc introduced his *Constitutions*. In some monasteries, Lanfranc's *Constitutions* were adopted wholesale and led to a simplification of the elaborate Anglo-Saxon rite. At Ely, however, there is some reason to think that they were resisted by the new Norman community. Its leaders came from Jumièges and St Ouen at Rouen, where ancient practices similar to those

of the English *Regularis Concordia* had persisted after the establishment of the duchy of Normandy. Sympathy for Ely's pre-Conquest traditions and an independence of mind is implicit in Theodwine of Jumièges's insistence that the treasures of the Saxon church confiscated by William should be returned. Things may possibly have begun to change with the arrival of Abbot Richard in 1100. He came from Bec, the Norman monastery whose austere liturgy inspired Lanfranc's *Constitutions*.

The use of the tribune level

The research of Arnold Klukas on the use of the tribune (the great second-storey gallery) in Romanesque churches has sharpened our understanding of the impact of liturgy on architectural form. He has pointed out that the *Regularis Concordia* required three altars on the axis of the church: one at the east end, one in the nave and one at the west end. As there was usually an entrance at the west end, this chapel would have to be raised above it. The requirement for boys to sing antiphonally at the end of the mass from outside the enclosure of the monastic choir suggests a requirement for raised platforms to the north and south of the crossing. Finally, there may have been a general need for extra chapels above the ground floor in which the numerous ordained monks of large communities could celebrate private masses. Reference in the *Regularis Concordia* to devotions in the 'secret oratories of the church' may also refer to these remote upper chapels.

The tribune at Ely was therefore intended to have a liturgical life of its own. Early Norman Ely may have had several chapels. At the east end the main apse would have been flanked by a pair of two-storey chapels. In the main transepts there would have been six chapels on the ground floor and there was also space for six upstairs if necessary. The original broad bridges of the transept ends provided the places for choirs to sing antiphonally (within sight of the monks in their stalls) and would permit dignified processions around the upper church.

The use of the west front

The upper chapels of the west transepts were approached from the ground floor by handsomely proportioned staircases and passageways. If the monks had continued to use the upper levels at the east end, this would mean that they had sites for over twenty altars. As the funding crisis caused by the creation of the bishopric in 1109 reduced the size of the community from a projected seventy monks to forty, this looks like over-provision.

It seems possible, therefore, that the demolition of the transept bridges signalled that extensive liturgical use of the upper church was to be discontinued in favour of the four chapels at the west end. At Rochester, where the cathedral had accepted Lanfranc's reforms long before, the tribune gallery of the nave was built as a purely decorative feature, without a floor. Closer to home, in the much earlier nave at Thorney abbey where Abbot Gunther had promoted similar austerities, there are signs that this may also have been so. But why did the monks not simply leave the broad bridges of the main transepts in their original form, as they did at Winchester? In the south transept at Ely the bridge enclosed a dark and uninviting space where the adjacent monks' dormitory ruled out the possibility of windows. In the north transept the translation of the benefactors provided a new devotional focus in an area which by the later Middle Ages at any rate appears to have been the principal approach for pilgrims. Both these considerations may have prompted the demolition of the bridges, which after this date were never again to feature in English church design.

What route would be taken by the ordained monks who now needed to celebrate in the

27. A Tournai marble grave slab discovered below the floor of St Mary's church in the nineteenth century. It is usually associated with Bishop Nigel, whose burial in 1169 fits the style. A large figure of the archangel Michael holds, in a napkin, the soul of the departed whose little pastoral staff implies a bishop or prior.

chapels of the west front? In order to reach this part of the church they would almost certainly have made frequent use of the lavish entrance from the cloister to the nave south aisle which we call – for no very good reason – the Prior's Door (Fig. 24). No surviving Anglo-Norman abbey has a western cloister door with such splendid sculptural decoration. But then only Ely has such a rich and elaborately equipped west end.

The west front had also a secondary function as the bishop's entrance to the church. The entry itself was made through an arch a few metres above the ground in the south façade of the south-west transept. When Bishop Eustace (1197–1215) granted the monks permission to build a cellar on his land, he stipulated that it could be built between the refectory and 'the wall of the passage by which one goes from our dwelling-house to the church'. The lavish and festive character of the south-west transept may be partly explained by its use as the episcopal entrance. Certainly, notwithstanding the loss of the northern limb, the splendid interior composition with the elaborate western lantern rising above the transepts is still best experienced from the bishop's approach.

The death of Nigel

Bishop Nigel suffered a stroke and died on 30 May 1169. He was buried next to the altar of the Holy Cross, at the east end of the nave *(Fig. 27)*. In this he may have been following the precedent of Hervey who, as one text of the *Liber Eliensis* ambiguously records, was buried 'before the cross'. Later bishops, some of whom

were to play a decisive role in the building and decoration of the church, were buried further east, where they lay in close proximity to the bodies of the saints and under the protection of their intercession. Why then were Hervey and Nigel interred in the lay part of the church, before the entrance to the monks' choir? Perhaps they, and other Norman bishops like Walkelin of Winchester, were following the humility of the early popes, buried in their atrium at the entrance to Old St Peter's, as it were before the gates of heaven.

The pulpitum

The gates to the monks' choir were set in a substantial screen known as the pulpitum. Ely's pulpitum was destroyed in the later eighteenth century, which is a pity because it was the earliest to survive in England to that date. The design was reconstructed by W.H. St John Hope in 1917 from the eighteenth-century sketches of James Essex *(Fig. 28)*. It is an interesting design with originally a pair of doorways intended to

28. The pulpitum (a reconstruction of 1917 by W.H. St John Hope based on the mid-eighteenth-century sketches of James Essex). This major liturgical division between the monks' choir and the nave was destroyed in the great reordering of 1770–1.

flank the altar of the Holy Cross. Missing areas of limewash on the second pair of nave piers show exactly where it once stood, as do early plans (see Plan 2). The pulpitum must have been built shortly after the burial of Bishop Nigel. The details are very similar to those found in the clerestory of the west front, which is known to have been completed by his successor.

BISHOP RIDEL AND THE BUILDING OF THE WEST TOWER

On the death of Nigel in 1169, the temporary custody of the see was given to Geoffrey Ridel. This ambitious man was already keeper of the Great Seal and a close confidant of Henry II. Six years earlier he had been appointed archdeacon of Canterbury and had used this position to promote a campaign against Thomas Becket, his archbishop. Becket excommunicated his archdeacon, or 'our archdevil of Canterbury' as he once described him, in the year of Nigel's death. Ridel was not to be enthroned until 1174, three years after the death of Becket.

The completion of the west front

The chronicler records that Ridel repaired the damage done to the shrine of Etheldreda by Nigel and 'nearly completed the new work to the west with the tower right to the top' *(Fig. 22)*. In the third design phase of the west front the arrival of the gothic style is announced by its leitmotiv, the pointed arch. There is also an analogous development in the moulded sections

30. The different arcade rhythms of adjacent storeys overlap in the south-west turret.

29. (left) South-west transept. The gothic arches of the clerestory are the work of Bishop Ridel (1274–89). The second tier of arcading (c.1130–40) was originally open but was filled in as a later precaution. In some later façades (e.g. Wells and Salisbury) openings at this level are known to have been used for singers in the Palm Sunday liturgy.

of arches, where cylindrical rolls are replaced by pointed 'keels'. The huge, richly ornamented arches of the western crossing are pointed and there are other new gothic details in the south-west transept clerestory, in the stumpy arcade beneath and in the upper parts of its tribune.

For much of his life Ridel was travelling in France. Here he must have seen some of the first buildings put up in the new gothic style. In 1164 he was certainly at Sens where he would have beheld the new cathedral that was one of the landmarks of early gothic. His work at Ely shows considerable originality and, not surprisingly, direct knowledge of advanced French work.

Anglo-Norman Romanesque began as a logical system in which bays and storeys are clearly separated. Ridel's west-front turrets, however, play a more adventurous game. The individuality of the bay is compromised by interpenetrating the storeys so that the ascending shafts of one layer run straight through the middle of the arches in the next *(Fig. 30)*. In the south-west tower of Chartres cathedral (begun 1142) – a building which Ridel may well have known – we can observe exactly the same tendencies. In all cases, however, the Chartres mason simply omitted shafts and buttresses to maintain the integrity of the individual layers *(Fig. 32)*. Ridel's mason on the other hand enjoyed the counterpoint of different rhythms and in this he anticipated some of the eccentricities of thirteenth-century English gothic.

The outside of the great west tower seems conventional enough, achieving its great height through multiple layers of niches and windows, alternating short and tall. The approach is typical of the French gothic of the Soissonaise region and is close in feeling to the south transept at Noyon (1170–85) and the choir at Chars (*c.*1190). Internally, however, the first three storeys are given over to a lantern whose design is a great surprise and delight *(Fig. 31)*. Here the plain gothic windows of the exterior are overlain internally with slender shafts. These are built two deep and placed so that the three openings of the interior subdivide the single external window. The rhythm of three against one and the doubling of the shafts create an exciting spatial effect: a remarkable exploitation of the Norman thick-wall building tradition in which this elaborate tower is entirely constructed.

31. West tower lantern (after 1174). Although its heavy structure is Romanesque, the use of pointed arches and screens of delicate pillars is related to the latest developments of early gothic architecture in France. (National Monuments Record)

But if there is much to admire in this late twelfth-century work, there are also some baffling signs of ineptitude. The repeat ornament of the external transept walls is a technical disaster. It begins as a triangle in relief and modulates into other patterns as it rises. Compared with the masterly treatment of a similar device on the west front of Castle Acre priory, the Ely work is out of control. The pattern cannot be regular when each triangle is determined by the width of its stone, whatever that width happens to be. This chaotic technique, somewhat modified, overrides the design change between the second (ornamented Romanesque) and third (gothic) phase. It suggests that if new French concepts arrived with Ridel's master mason, they were carried out by a local team with its own way of doing things. This paradox is borne out by recent research on the responsibilities of master masons, which argues that whereas some masons determined every detail, others had a looser connection with the execution of their ideas.

One important early gothic feature of the transepts was the steep angle of the original roofs. Their former profile is clearly seen in the masonry on both sides of the tower and can be contrasted with the lower pitch of the Norman nave roof. At the same time, the turrets would have been given steep, conical caps. But what of the main tower itself? The monastic chronicle, in the version quoted, makes it clear that Ridel nearly finished it. We may wonder what he left incomplete.

The tower interior shows clear signs that Ridel intended to finish it with an octagon, a scheme which has Romanesque precedents and contemporary early gothic parallels *(Fig. 32)*. At the top the internal corners of the tower are bridged by contemporary half-round arches or 'squinches'. These create a stout octagonal base on which the present, much slighter, western octagon was built many years later. The tower of St Mary's at Swaffham Prior, close to Ely, is

32. The south tower of Chartres (begun 1142) displays rhythmic differences between storeys like those of the turret tops at Ely and the spire sits on an octagonal drum similar to the one that Ridel intended for his great west tower.

contemporary with Ridel's work. It has the same squinches, which there support the octagonal middle section of its very unusual top. It is clear that a western octagon was planned at Ely long before the present late fourteenth-century top was contemplated. As we shall see, there is some reason to suppose that it was completed in the early years of the thirteenth century and then given a very substantial wooden spire.

Changes at the east end

While the west tower was rising, changes to which the bishop also made a significant contribution were taking place in the choir. The pul-

pitum was contemporary with Ridel's western work, but it was probably not funded by the bishop as the chronicler does not mention it. But Ridel was involved in other ways. He covered two sides and the top of the principal shrine with silver; and also paid for the painting of the middle part of the choir and of the 'throne of the high altar' (*cathedram magni altaris*). The word *cathedra* means 'bishop's throne', and it is specified as of the high altar to distinguish it from his normal seat in the western part of the choir. It seems likely that the painting was done for Ridel's enthronement in 1174.

It may have been at this time that the great early Norman apse in which the shrines stood was demolished and made square, an alteration that was revealed in the excavation undertaken by Robert Willis in 1850. Square east ends are characteristic of late twelfth-century English architecture and there are other signs in the south presbytery aisle of a late Romanesque remodelling of the choir before the great rebuilding of Bishop Northwold. The late twelfth century was one of the most active building periods in the history of Ely and Ridel's work at the cathedral needs to be set in the context of a wide-ranging renovation of the monastery undertaken at this time *(see Figs. 33 and 34)*.

RIDEL'S SUCCESSORS

In 1189 Bishop William Longchamp, chancellor and regent of England during the absence of Richard I, was enthroned as bishop. He died in 1197, while on a diplomatic mission to Rome,

33. (right) The richly varied arches of the infirmary arcade (c.1170–80) are closely comparable to Ridel's work on the west front but more refined in execution. (From G. Millers, A Description of the Cathedral Church of Ely, *1834)*

34. The interior of the infirmary chapel has the earliest rib vault at Ely. Construction is simplified by the ribs, which require minimal timber centring. Between them thin webs of stone can do the job of the former massive groin vaults (Fig. 13). *(From G. Millers,* A Description of the Cathedral Church of Ely, *1834)*

and was buried near Poitiers in France. If he contributed anything to the building apart from a lost marble tomb for his heart, it is not recorded. He bequeathed money and some interesting relics. These included phials of the oil of the sepulchres of St Mary and of St Demetrius, teeth of St Peter and some precious metalwork.

He was followed by Eustace, successively keeper of the Great Seal and chancellor, who held the see until 1215. Eustace is credited with the building – or rebuilding – of St Mary's parish church, whose delicate nave arcades and ornate north door closely resemble Ridel's work at the cathedral. It is also recorded that Eustace 'built the new Galilee from the foundations towards the west'. Several writers have found it difficult to reconcile a date before 1215 with the very sophisticated gothic detail of the present Galilee porch. This difficult issue will be deferred until we have assessed the magnificent works at Ely associated with that great bishop and builder Hugh de Northwold.

4. BISHOP NORTHWOLD AND THE TRANSFORMATION OF THE CATHEDRAL

Bishop Northwold, elected in 1229, initiates a series of major additions and alterations. He builds a new western spire in about 1230, and in 1234 adds a great six-bay presbytery to the east end of the choir. This building, finished in 1252, is an outward expression of the shrine of Etheldreda. Its design and decoration speak of her relationship with the Virgin Mary. Much of the surviving painted decoration at Ely belongs to this period in which the Galilee porch was also brought to completion.

Eustace had died in 1215, the year of Magna Carta, which set out a reduction of the king's authority that was followed by civil war and invasion by the French prince, Louis. Ely's powerful position attracted King John's enemies, who took possession of the isle only to be ousted by the king's forces, who were able to cross the ice in strength in the freezing winter of early 1216. The cathedral was desecrated in the course of this action.

A BISHOP AMONG BISHOPS

Bishop Hugh of Northwold followed the brief episcopates of Eustace's successors, John of Fountains (1220–5) and Geoffrey de Burgh (1225–8). These two are not known to have built anything, but De Burgh gilded the upper part of St Etheldreda's shrine and contributed some precious silver discs for the making of its gabled roof. Northwold was abbot of the great

monastery at Bury St Edmunds before he was enthroned as bishop of Ely in 1229. In spite of an active rôle in politics, he wore throughout his life the simple black habit of a Benedictine monk. His contemporary, Matthew Paris, called him 'the flower of the Benedictine order, shining brilliantly as an abbot among abbots, as a bishop among bishops; profuse in his hospitality and at table maintaining a calm cheerfulness which attracted all beholders'. It was during Northwold's episcopate that the cathedral was to be decisively transformed from an evocation of antique Roman grandeur into a more transcendent image of the Heavenly Jerusalem.

Northwold was responsible for the building of the remarkable new presbytery *(Figs. 37 and 52)* at the east end. He also built a spire on the west tower, and put up a new hall and treasury at the bishop's palace. His funds may have been limited to these projects (see p. **58**), but it is evident that his energy drove a more wide-ranging series of alterations.

35. Bishop Northwold's counter seal of c.1229 may show the timber and lead spire that he added to the west tower. (Cambridge University Library)

The western spire

Northwold's addition to the west tower was evidently a substantial undertaking because Matthew Paris in his description of the consecration of the presbytery refers to it in passing as *hoc turrim excelentissimam* (that most excellent tower). The monastic chronicle records that Northwold 'newly constructed the wooden tower [or steeple] towards the Galilee from the masons' work to the top'. At least one translation reverses the sense of the last part turning 'from the masons' work' (*ab opere cementario*) into 'out of stonework', as though a wooden top

had been replaced by a stone one. Such are the ambiguities of translation but, on balance, it seems most likely that Northwold's top was of wood with a lead covering. Although demolished in the fourteenth century, it may not be entirely lost because the bishop's seal seems to record its appearance *(Fig. 35)*.

The bishop's seal

One side of the seal has the standing figure of the bishop vested for the mass and with his right hand raised in benediction. The reverse, the 'counter seal', is more complex. Northwold's devotion to St Edmund and to St Etheldreda is expressed here in two figures which stand on either side of a beautifully proportioned spire, beneath which is a small kneeling donor figure of the bishop himself. At the top of the spire St Peter holds the keys. The whole arrangement is quite unlike the general run of bishops' seals. The surprisingly modern perspective rendering of the steeple has a forerunner in the depiction of city churches in the early gothic seal of the barons of London (*c.*1219).

The tower on which the spire stands is a simplified image of the west tower, with a pointed window surmounted by a bull's eye as its top storey. It is as though the goldsmith who made the seal matrix had taken one of the corner elements of Ridel's tower to represent the building as a whole. The spire itself is slender, elegant and embellished with crockets. It is flanked by well-proportioned corner pinnacles standing on tall turrets. The height of these corner turrets is distinctive. It implies that, as in the early gothic south tower at Chartres *(Fig. 32)* and the central tower at Coutances in Normandy, they may have embraced an octagonal drum of the same height on which, at Ely, the spire proper was built. As the seal must date from just after Northwold's enthronement in 1229, the western spire will have been one of his earliest projects at the cathedral.

36. All Saints, Elm, Cambridgeshire (early thirteenth century and later). This great thirteenth-century parish church served a settlement which grew in the first half of the thirteenth century as large areas of new farmland were won from the surrounding fen by tenants of the bishops of Ely.

37. St Mary's, Long Sutton, Lincolnshire: tower and spire (mid-thirteenth century). This famous marshland church lies just over the border of the medieval diocese. Its important timber spire may emulate Bishop Northwold's steeple at Ely, a suggestion first made by Gilbert Scott.

Local echoes of the thirteenth-century steeple

A great work like this would have been likely to have some impact on the architecture of the locality. An intriguing local group of thirteenth-century steeples may be directly relevant to the western composition at Ely. Firstly, there is Barnack *(Fig. 7)*, where the Saxon tower has a

thirteenth-century octagonal top with a low spire – if spire is the right word to describe what is more of a stone roof. Built in a very similar style is the contemporary western tower of Elm *(Fig. 36)*, which is clearly thirteenth century, but bears an uncanny resemblance to the present, later western octagon at Ely.

45

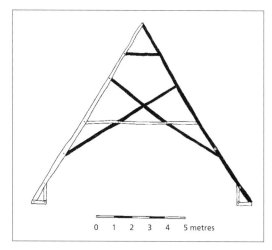

0 1 2 3 4 5 metres

38. The design of the thirteenth-century nave roof (c.1240). Reused twelfth-century timbers in this bay are shown in black. (After Gavin Simpson)

Finally there is at Long Sutton, Lincolnshire, an octagonal lead-covered spire with pinnacles raised on four tall corner turrets *(Fig. 37)*. This magnificent structure looks very like a small version of the spire shown on the seal and is the oldest and most impressive timber spire in England. At Sutton we can see that the lead and timber have to be read as one composition with the masonry of the storey immediately beneath. So it may be that the curious description of the monastic chronicler, 'from the masons' work to the top', was intended to distinguish Northwold's contribution from a similar group of octagon and embracing turrets at Ely. The 'masons' work' may have been an octagonal stone superstructure with which the monks had completed Ridel's tower in the early years of the thirteenth century, perhaps with a conical roof similar to the stone one at Barnack.

The nave roof

The herringbone pattern of the lead at Long Sutton is an authentic feature and a similar pattern survived on the roof of Ely's nave until the nineteenth century. The nave roof is one of the great thirteenth-century contributions at Ely. It has the fashionable steep pitch of the early gothic period (as at Lincoln and Salisbury) and its construction was part of a general re-roofing of the cathedral. Its scissor-brace structure makes use of a multitude of relatively slender timbers which, with additional braces, define the semi-octagonal underside that was to prove such a good shape for the application of the Victorian boarded ceiling and its paintings *(Fig. 38)*. The growth rings of these timbers have given a felling date of *c.*1240. With the building of the presbytery the same type of roof (recorded in a drawing by James Essex) was added at the east end, while on the ends of the main transepts new stone spires crowned the corner turrets *(Figs. 12, 53 and 71)*. It is possible that the old Norman crossing tower, which collapsed early in the following century, also received some further attention at this time but there is, of course, no evidence. In general terms, however, the rather blunt and boxy Norman silhouette of the cathedral had now been transformed into an assembly of acutely pointed prismatic shapes.

THE NEW PRESBYTERY

The crowning achievement of Northwold's life was the new presbytery, which he began in 1234 and completed in 1252. At the service at which the bishop dedicated 'the whole church of Ely' to St Mary, St Peter and St Etheldreda on the anniversary of Etheldreda's translation in 1252, the saints' relics were solemnly moved once more. The new work, which had involved the demolition of the former square east end, extended the choir in six new bays of unprecedented richness *(Col. pl. 5)*.

The dedication and translation were witnessed by a glittering company including Henry III, the Lord Edward, the bishops of Llandaff and Norwich and 'many magnates of the realm,

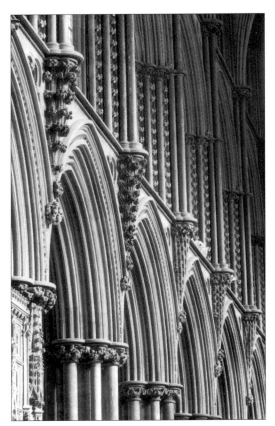

39. The changing form of the carved brackets in the presbytery may relate to the site of the shrine.

local saints and what was then thought to be the body of St Alban, England's first martyr, which had been in the church since the early eleventh century (see p. **61**). There were other lesser relics and a series of side altars, the most important of which was the chapel of the Blessed Virgin Mary. This occupied the western half of the south aisle.

Finally, there was Northwold himself. He seems to have selected the key position for his tomb at the feet of Etheldreda *(Fig. 41)*. There would also have been a place for his episcopal throne. This is very likely to be the great stone seat of which one side survives in the cathedral. Crouching on the arm rest is the figure of a wolf holding between its paws the head of St Edmund, as it was discovered after his martyrdom. The martyrdom itself is depicted in a relief at the feet of the bishop's effigy, which lies in a canopied surround decorated with figures of saints. So there may have been a central group of three important objects. The shrine lay beneath the boss of Etheldreda on the high vault *(Fig. 44)*. The tomb of Northwold lay to its east and perhaps the throne lay east of the tomb, under the boss with the enthroned Virgin. Bishop Durandus, writing in late thirteenth-century France, recommends that an episcopal throne should be dedicated 'to the honour of apostles and martyrs, and especially of the Virgin Mary'.

also prelates and innumerable clerks', according to Matthew Paris. Northwold – who was heard to declare, like the aged Simeon of the gospels, 'Lord, now lettest thou thy servant depart in peace' – may have been thinking of the fate of Abbot Richard (see p. **23**). For the first time Etheldreda's name had been included in the dedication of the church and, as Peter Draper has made clear, Northwold's presbytery was designed specifically to give her shrine a setting of unparalleled magnificence.

The contents of the presbytery

Around the principal shrine and its altar it was necessary to provide sites for other important objects and functions. These included the other

The Heavenly Jerusalem

It has long been recognised that one of the important symbolic objectives of the gothic cathedral was to stand as an image of the Heavenly Jerusalem. The text that fired the imagination of the medieval builders and their patrons was the book of Revelation – or the Apocalypse, as it was more popularly known. In this extraordinary work the writer, John, conjures images of bizarre beauty and events of great violence that precede the Last Judgement

40. One of the remaining gargoyles of Bishop Northwold's presbytery. The water-vomiting fiend clutches a naked human figure. Apart from three vault bosses and a series of fine heads hidden in the clerestory, the figure sculpture of this serene architecture is chiefly grotesque.

and describes its sequel, the creation of the New Jerusalem.

The Apocalypse was a particularly popular text in Northwold's time and the subject of a large number of glorious manuscripts made for rich secular patrons. These manuscripts incorporated commentaries that expanded its meaning and attempted to unlock the secret of its mysterious numbers and symbols. The popular commentary of Joachim of Fiori picked out the 1,260 days of prophecy described in Chapter 11 and predicted that the third and final era of human history would begin in the year 1260. This was eight years, as it happened, after the completion of Northwold's building. The passage from Revelation designated for the dedication of a new church includes these words:

I saw a new heaven and a new earth: for the first heaven and the first earth are passed away and the sea is no more. And I saw the holy city, new Jerusalem, coming down out of heaven from God, made ready as a bride is adorned for her husband. (Revelation 21.1, 2)

The Virgin Mary

As well as conveying this general image the architecture of the presbytery may have carried a more specific symbolic message. The cult of the Virgin Mary was by then one of the most powerful themes in Christian spirituality. In medieval theology and art the Church is always construed as female. Twelfth-century scholars at Chartres moreover had promoted the idea that the New Jerusalem was to be interpreted as the Virgin Mary, who would reign as queen of heaven. Another architectural image occurs in Revelation: 'And there was opened the temple of God that is in heaven' (11.19). In the magnificent Apocalypse manuscript commissioned by the Lord Edward about fifteen years after his attendance at Ely's dedication, the temple is shown as a contemporary gothic building *(Fig. 42)*. It contains a shrine-like ark and is surrounded by creatures like gargoyles whose mouths vomit fire and hail. The ninth-century commentary of Berengaudus, which forms a sub-text in this manuscript, explains that the temple can also be understood as the Blessed Mary and that the ark is Christ who assumed flesh from her.

In one sense, therefore, the whole of the presbytery at Ely could be seen to embody the idea of the Virgin Mary. How is this idea conveyed and where does Etheldreda fit into the picture? The obvious connection between Mary and Ely's royal saint is expressed in the bosses of the high vault. Here the central boss is the Coronation of the Virgin. The Virgin, crowned by Christ, presides over the whole Heavenly City and Etheldreda, enthroned as queen and saint,

42. A miniature from a manuscript of the Apocalypse commissioned by the Lord Edward (later Edward I) c.1270 (Oxford, Bodleian, MS Douce 180): 'And there was opened the temple of God that is in heaven' (Revelation 11.19). Northwold's presbytery is in part an architectural realisation of the images of the Heavenly Jerusalem described in Revelation. (Conway Library, Courtauld Institute of Art. Reproduced by permission of the Bodleian Library)

41. (above) Bishop Northwold's Purbeck marble effigy of c.1250 is surrounded by luxuriant foliage and figures of saints. (below) Northwold's devotion to St Edmund is shown in the relief of the saint's martyrdom, at the feet of his effigy. The stone fragment to the left may be a section of his episcopal throne, on whose armrest a crouching wolf holds Edmund's head between its paws.

is the only other figured boss on the ridge. The message could hardly be plainer. Etheldreda is a successor to the Virgin Mary as in Bede's hymn to the saint, which makes the same connection:

> Fair maid, who gav'st the whole world's Parent birth,
> God gave thee grace. And by that grace empowered
> How many virgin blossoms have since flowered!

There follows a list of early virgin saints, among whom Etheldreda takes her place.

> Our age at length in triumphs such as these
> Partakes through ETHELDREDA's victories.
> Queenly by birth, an earthly crown she wore
> Right nobly; but a heavenly pleased her more.

St Peter, the third dedication of the church, is the subject of the only other figured boss. He holds the keys and an image of the Church ('thou art Peter and upon this rock I will build my church'; Matthew 16.18). He is situated oddly off-centre towards the east, possibly to indicate the site of the relic contributed by Bishop Longchamp, or simply to commemorate the eastern dedication of the Saxon church. Peter is dressed as a Benedictine monk (following an Anglo-Saxon convention) and so makes the important connection between the theme of virginity of the principal bosses and the celibacy of the monastic community.

Carved foliage

If Etheldreda's boss accurately locates the former position of her shrine – immediately beneath it – this may have a bearing on the distribution and design of the magnificent foliage sculpture for which the presbytery is famous. The type of foliage, known as stiff-leaf, is very typical of early English gothic but the abundance of it at Ely is remarkable – particularly in the middle storey, where it sprouts between the shafts. These excesses were to be imitated in the angel choir at Lincoln, but at Ely they were perhaps endowed with particular significance. They are perhaps a celebration of Etheldreda's virginity and authority as it was symbolised in the miracle of the sprouting staff (see p. **6**).

More particularly, the magnificent brackets fixed between the arches of the main arcade *(Fig. 39)* can be seen to change their form as they approach and surround the site of the shrine. At the east end they are tightly furled in an unusual manner which denies their decorative purpose. But around the shrine, in the two western bays – where Etheldreda slept as she had done on that grassy bank in Lincolnshire six hundred years before – they miraculously burst forth.

Numbers

Everything in such a building was capable, in the medieval mind, of carrying numerological significance derived from a wide range of biblical sources. In the twelfth and thirteenth centuries, religious architecture was the subject of poetic and spiritual meditation informed by these special numbers. On either side of the presbytery at Ely there are two sets of seven pillars and responds. According to Durandus:

> the piers ... are called seven, according to the saying, 'Wisdom hath builded up her house, she hath hewn out her seven pillars.' [Proverbs 9.1] because bishops ought to be filled with the sevenfold influences of the Holy Ghost.

In 1218–20 the abbot of St Augustine's at Bristol needed the services of a skilled mason. He wrote to the dean of Wells asking him 'to release your servant L. to hew out the seven pillars of wisdom's house, meaning of course our chapel of the Blessed Virgin'. Bristol's elder Lady chapel does not even have major pillars and in this case, the abbot was speaking figuratively. If, moreover, the Virgin is to be identified with the New Jerusalem, then at Ely we might be tempted to see the twelve openings framed by the pillars as the twelve gates of the city.

But is it not possible to *superimpose* almost any kind of theological number framework onto this structure? Did not Abbot Suger at St Denis in the 1140s write of the twelve columns of his new apse as the apostles? Durandus indeed continues this game, calling the apostles pillars and doors, seeing the bases as the apostolic bishops and the capitals as the opinions of the bishops and doctors, and so on. These are in fact all legitimate thirteenth-century ways of responding to buildings, contradictory and overlapping though they might be. At Ely, however, it is conceivable that the Blessed Virgin is the figure upon which any meditation on numbers is intended to converge. For Northwold, the formidable Benedictine, and his celibate community the lavish presbytery may have been a celebration of the glories of chastity and its future heavenly reward.

ARCHITECTURAL DESIGN IN THE
PRESBYTERY

Vaults and buttresses

The theological messages are embodied in a building of remarkable sophistication in which the full gothic structural system appears at Ely for the first time. The cross-section of the Norman choir determined its height and the proportion of its individual storeys. The main space of the presbytery was now vaulted in stone and the vault needed an effective system of support. Thick-wall construction alone was incapable of resisting its outward thrust and so Northwold's mason adopted the flying buttresses that the French had developed in the previous century *(Figs. 43 and 67)*. The aisle walls are, for the first time at Ely, divided by deep, tower-like buttresses from whose inner faces two tiers of arches spring out to support the presbytery wall. The lower tier is intended to receive the thrust from the vault, and this

43. The section of the presbytery drawn by D.J. Stewart in 1868. On the right he shows the arrangement of Northwold's thirteenth-century flying buttresses (the pinnacle is, however, fourteenth century). On the left (in a darker tone) is the outline of the new buttresses which replaced most of them in the mid-fourteenth century (see p. 80).

51

44. The presbytery vault (c.1250). (National Monuments Record)

lateral movement is arrested by the compressive weight of the buttress tower. The upper arch is thinner and more elegant. It carries a beautifully formed channel for rainwater and no doubt helps to prevent the spreading of the roof. The steep new gothic roof shed water rapidly and the upper arches carried it straight to the throats of extraordinary creatures, which spewed it outwards to the ground like the hail-vomiting gargoyles of the Douce Apocalypse *(Figs. 40 and 42)*.

The lowest part of the buttress supports the vaults of the aisles. These are pure quadripartite rib vaults, so called because the diagonal ribs, between which the webs are built, divide the vault into four parts. The rib vault is the structural successor to the earlier and more primitive groin vault. The ribs are built first and then the webs are filled in. This makes construction easier and the pointed, transverse arches contribute to greater structural efficiency. The high vault is a good deal more complicated and decorative *(Fig. 44)*. A ridge rib runs down the centre and extra ribs called tiercerons rise up from the springers to meet it. Each bay also has a horizontal ridge rib running north–south and tiercerons rise to meet this as well. The resulting taut pattern of foliage bosses and ribs is a very English response to the decorative possibilities of rib vaulting. These ideas had been developed in the nave of Lincoln cathedral shortly before Northwold's building was begun.

The vault makes very elegant use of what the French call *tas-de-charge*. In this system the half-cone of springing vault ribs is built out in solid horizontal courses of masonry to limit the amount of vault that has to be built in ribs and webs. The Ely vault springers are particularly

45. The cantilevered horizontal masonry courses known as tas-de-charge *in the springings of the presbytery vault.*

MATERIALS AND FINISH

The quality of design and execution in the presbytery represents the high point of English early gothic. It is doubtful, for example, whether any English building has a more finely proportioned main arcade. There is something immensely satisfying in the way in which the handsome curves of the great arches, expressed in numerous deeply undercut mouldings, bear down on the glorious foliage capitals. Barnack limestone is used throughout the building. The webs of the vaults are made of clunch, a soft chalk quarried nearby at Burwell and Isleham. But many key features (piers, capitals, minor shafts and strings) are executed in dark Purbeck marble, a fossil-bearing stone brought by sea from the Dorset coast and made fashionable by the rebuilding of Canterbury after 1174.

The standard of finish in this thirteenth-century work is very striking especially in comparison with the heavy details of the Norman building, much of which would have been worked with the axe. Chisels of many different sorts began to be more widely used in the late twelfth century (see the lovely details of the infirmary) (Fig. 33). It is clear from the iron frames (ferramenta) of windows (Fig. 46) and other ornamental work that this period saw great advances in the use of metal. This must have included improvements in the tempering of tools to enable them to remain sharp and allow the wonderfully undercut mouldings and foliage of the presbytery. These striking improvements in masonry cutting are also obvious in the Galilee porch.

good examples of this technique *(Fig. 45)*. Here one can admire the finely jointed masonry (which in other buildings, like Salisbury and Lincoln, was a source of amazement to contemporaries) and marvel at the magnificent mouldings which create rib bundles, rising and separating in different planes and curves.

THE GALILEE PORCH

The use of the term 'Galilee' to describe a building at the west end of a great church is at least as old as a customary of 1035 which refers to one at the great abbey of Cluny in Burgundy. At Durham the Galilee is a low, wide chapel built onto the west front and at Lincoln it is a handsome porch on the west wall of the south transept. The exact meaning of the name is uncertain. It may refer to an outer space, 'the land beyond Jordan, Galilee of the Gentiles' (Matthew 4.15).

46. *Ferramenta of c.1240 from the east window of the presbytery, now in the north transept.*

St Pantaleon at Cologne (late tenth century), where a substantial porch is combined with western transepts. But there is no clear archaeological evidence of one at Ely and it has to be acknowledged that Anglo-Norman churches do not generally have porches. If they had Galilees, these would probably have been contrived with timber screens in the western bays of their typically long naves (filled-in sockets may be seen at Ely in the third and fourth pair of piers from the west). In the context of such an internal division Eustace's Galilee would have been new and the chronicler's assertion that it was built 'from the foundations towards the west' makes sense.

47. *The Galilee is recorded as having been built from the foundations by Bishop Eustace (1197–1215), but much of the architectural detail looks rather later, suggesting a certain amount of rebuilding or remodelling.*

Ely's double-storey Galilee is one of the finest thirteenth-century porches in England (*Figs. 47 and 48*). Some early writers have been content to ascribe the whole of the present structure to Eustace while others have doubted whether its sophisticated gothic architecture could have been built before the bishop's death in 1215. James Bentham, writing in the mid-eighteenth century, was the first modern author to acknowledge the probable existence at Ely of a Galilee earlier than the present one. What Eustace built before 1215 was, after all, called a *new* Galilee, so there must have been an earlier one. It is therefore tempting to imagine an earlier projecting Galilee, and examples of comparable buildings in the early Romanesque architecture of Germany come to mind, notably

The design

When we look at the plan of the cathedral the immense thickness of the porch walls is very striking. Externally it means that the outer flanks could be treated as continuous arcading unin- terrupted by the buttresses that the inter- nal vaults would otherwise have required. Substantial keeled shaft bundles form the corners, but the horizontal registers of the sides carry through to the front façade. Here the arches, which have now become niches for sculp- ture, are scooped into bold concave curves.

Inside the porch the massive wall thickness allows a grand composition of deep arcades *(Fig. 48)*. Rising from the bench, a screen of tre- foiled arches houses a raised sill on which another arcade follows a syncopated rhythm. The two are linked together by a little stone vault that supports the second, pillared level of the porch interior. The thin iron struts are part of the original structure incorporated to prevent the spreading of the miniature vault during construction.

It is normal to contrast the spatial ambition of early French gothic with the more simple rectilinear planning of early English, but in buildings like the Ely Galilee English masons found their spatial drama in the wall itself. The sumptuous inner portal is a remodelling of the earlier entrance and its inward reveals are twelfth century. If the vaulted porch is without equal in its elegance and richness, the chamber above (unroofed in the eighteenth century) is by contrast plain and utilitarian. It can only have been used very occasionally.

The date of the Galilee porch

Although the porch gives the appearance of a purposeful and unified design, careful exam- ination of the masonry coursing and other details implies various changes of mind and the possibility that work of more than one period is involved. The decorative arcades of the outer

48. Galilee interior.

side walls show various changes of detail and the vault of the interior uses two different rib sections. If Eustace completed his Galilee before 1215, this structure may have received further attention, perhaps twenty years later, during the period when the cathedral was being comprehensively overhauled under the leader- ship of Bishop Northwold. This cannot be a categorical statement, but if architecture as delicate and complex as the western niches of the Galilee is dated to the beginning of the century, that suggests that there was no signifi- cant development in English gothic between 1215 and 1235. In 1868 Canon David Stewart made a similar point and, in spite of more recent comparisons with the prodigious novel- ties in St Hugh's choir at Lincoln (begun *c.*1192), Stewart's argument that the moulded detail is in places more advanced than that of

Northwold's choir holds good. It is true that the syncopated wall arcades appear to have been invented in the early Lincoln work, but the planning of those in the Galilee porch is closer to fragments identified as part of the new base which Northwold built for the shrine of St Etheldreda.

The use of the porch

The porch would have had several roles to play, but it was not perhaps the much-used entrance to the cathedral that it is today. Covered space at the west doors was useful because of the ceremonies that were performed there. The Palm Sunday procession, carrying an ark with relics and a pyx containing the Blessed Sacrament, would, after its tour of the town, return to the church and halt at the west door. The Sacrament was about to re-enact Christ's triumphant entry into Jerusalem. In the Sarum Use, of which the earliest copies date from the mid-thirteenth century, the procession was met by a choir of boys (the children who carried palms and cried 'Hosannah in the highest').

The same requirement is found in the earlier Benedictine *Constitutions* of Lanfranc. He writes that when the procession comes to the doors of the church, it should halt with the children drawn up between the rows of the choir of monks. The shrine with the relics and the pyx should be set down here on a table covered with a rich cloth. A similar ceremony is known to have taken place at Peterborough in the thirteenth century. The spacious Galilee porch would have been well suited for this purpose and for the reception of important guests who, Lanfranc states, should be received outside the west door. Bishops are to be greeted with holy water, incense and a gospel book while the bells are rung. One can imagine the royal party and the bishops pausing here before making their way to the presbytery in the autumn of 1252. Although there is no evidence that Northwold

49. *Drawings of c.1250 scratched on the inner walls of the Galilee.*

paid for this work, it is interesting that of the two internal carved heads one is a small bishop above and between the inner doors.

Graffiti in the Galilee

A mid-thirteenth-century date for the completion of the Galilee seems to be confirmed by the very interesting architectural graffiti that survive on the smooth ashlar of its inner walls. On the south side at low level there are small incised designs for window tracery, gables and a shrine-like structure *(Fig. 49)*. On the north wall at the same height there are some trefoiled arches, and higher up is a little gable design enclosing a five-foiled arch. It was common for areas of a great church to be used as a temporary drawing office or 'tracing house' by the master mason before they were brought into liturgical use. At Ely the Galilee walls would have been covered in a thin coat of plaster on which the mason would have incised the designs with dividers and a metal scriber. The random scattering of individual designs and compass arcs are merely those that accidentally penetrated areas of thin plaster. Some of the drawings seem to represent unfinished or unresolved designs so what we have here is a precious record of the master mason's creative process.

Some designs may have been intended for tombs, shrines or screens in the new presbytery. One, for example, resembles the decorative niches around the effigy of Bishop Northwold *(Fig. 41)* (which, like the shrine, would perhaps have been commissioned around 1250). Drawings at this upper level could only have been made from scaffolding, as it is neither comfortable nor safe to work while standing on the masonry shelf. The most likely moment for the use of the Galilee as a drawing office was when building work still precluded its use as an entrance, perhaps during its completion.

The drawings of window tracery are particularly important. To understand their significance it is necessary only to compare the windows of the dark cloister *(Fig. 71)* with the three windows inserted in the south transept chapels in the 1260s or 1270s *(Fig. 50)*. The dark cloister has what the Victorians called 'plate

50. A window of one of the south transept chapels (c.1260–70).

tracery', in which it appears that the wall has been perforated by a series of separate openings to create a pleasing pattern. The new windows of the transept chapels by contrast have fully developed 'bar tracery', in which the arches and other foiled shapes have been nudged together so closely that masonry is reduced to a skeletal framework of mouldings. This is the type of tracery scratched on the walls of the Galilee.

Tracery was soon to supersede the great lancet windows of early English gothic which make such a splendid showing in the east wall at Ely and it was used exclusively in Henry III's rebuilding of Westminster abbey (1245–69). The famous Angel Choir at Lincoln, begun in 1256, although heavily indebted to the Ely work in other ways, now rejected lancets in favour of tracery.

Because of this, more than one recent

account of Northwold's presbytery suggests that the building was old-fashioned by the standards of its contemporaries. But that is a modern view and not one which would necessarily have been understood by Northwold's peers. Matthew Paris, an artist and monastic chronicler from a rival Benedictine house, gave a contemporary opinion when he called it 'very costly and admirable work'. Costly it certainly was. Northwold is recorded to have spent more than £5,040 on the presbytery and between the years 1239 and 1250, for which some summary accounts survive, his contributions amounted to 75 per cent of the total funds. In the deployment of architectural ornament the thirteenth-century work in the presbytery and in the Galilee set a standard that would never be entirely eclipsed by subsequent fashions. It is clear, moreover, that well into the following century, when the Ely masons represented the cutting edge of architectural innovation in Europe, these great works were held in high regard. Their details inspired some of the more sophisticated aspects of the fourteenth-century work (see *Fig. 62* and p. **75**).

PAINTED DECORATION IN THE THIRTEENTH CENTURY

Much of the remaining painted decoration in the nave and transepts seems to date from the thirteenth century when, as we have seen, the church was comprehensively renovated and extended. In the south transept the walls and vaults were given an overall masonry pattern: this time the joints were indicated in black and one or two details were picked out in reds, greens and blues. In the vault of the clergy vestry (visible above the wall from the main body of the transept) this scheme was boldly 'restored' in the nineteenth century. The rather bright blue paint of the reliefs on the Norman capitals, and the picking out of the voussoirs in

the same colour is also a restoration but one apparently based on reliable evidence. In several places the original decoration can be seen quite clearly and the combination of masonry pattern with a border of leaf trails has a close counterpart in the thirteenth-century decoration of Durham's nave. The impact of the decoration in its original state is well conveyed in the watercolours made by that great pioneer of wall-painting studies, E.W. Tristram (*Col. pl. 6*). The eastern bays of the nave were treated in a similar fashion to the south transept. Coursed masonry was painted on the groin vaults and rather unconvincing painted ribs were added to the angles to bring them up to date. The arches here were lavishly decorated with spirals and chevrons, probably to give emphasis to the sanctuary of the nave altar.

The chapels of the north transept preserve the remains of some impressive schemes. The drum pier, which separates two of them, was covered in lozenge diaper work above a dado of hanging drapery. The arch of St Edmund's chapel has the remains of a series of roundels depicting saints, one of whom has recently been identified as St Lawrence with the gridiron on which he was martyred. The lower walls of both chapels were painted to look as though they were hung with expensive woven cloths. In the case of St George's chapel, where the paintings are now hidden behind the war memorial boards, the cloth has a woven pattern of encircled crouching dragons, whereas in St Edmund's chapel there are two depictions of patterned cloths: one decorated with barbed vertical stripes and the other an arrangement of mysterious discs. Hanging cloth designs like those in St George's chapel are found in the thirteenth-century nave of West Walton church, where great painted roundels seem to replicate some of the ornate masonry of Northwold's choir. The one remaining figure subject is the large lunette showing the martyrdom of St Edmund. In the course of recent conservation work a faint but menacing devil came to light low down on the central column of the gallery opening above this chapel. In this position it may represent Tutivillus, the listening devil who compiles records of reprehensible conversations and notes down inadequate and gabbled performances of the mass for reference on Judgement Day.

The painted decoration of Northwold's presbytery is a subject that would benefit from further research. It would appear that colour was used in a very restrained way. The painting of the vault, in which colour is restricted to ribs near the main bosses, is Victorian but this treat-ment is corroborated by medieval paint in the aisle vaults. One can imagine a scheme in which limited quantities of red, green and probably gold were used to highlight specific decorative features against a white limestone or clunch field with dark brown Purbeck performing an almost calligraphic function. It is an arrangement of tone and colour that is found in the contemporary pale line and wash of manuscripts by Matthew Paris and his school.

51. *The tomb of Bishop de Luda (1290–8). The monument was originally painted in strong colours. These were carefully reproduced on the side facing the choir during Gilbert Scott's reordering of 1847–52. The tomb chest was cut through to make an arch in the 1770s.*

LATER THIRTEENTH-CENTURY BISHOPS AND THEIR WORK

Northwold died in 1254, leaving the residue of his estate for the maintenance of the new work. His successor, William of Kilkenny, died in 1256 on an embassy to King Alfonso of Spain. His heart was buried in the presbytery 'on the north side between the pillars' and he has a fine effigy. Hugh of Balsham had a much longer episcopate, at the beginning of which war returned to Ely. In 1258–9 the baronial opposition to Henry III held the isle for a short while, until dry weather in July allowed the king's forces to cross the fen and drive them out. Balsham played an important part in the early development of the University of Cambridge by founding Peterhouse in 1284. In doing so he was participating in a movement by which colleges would eventually supplant monasteries like Ely as centres of learning. At his death in 1286 he was buried before the high altar and it has been suggested by Phillip Lindley that the beautiful headless bishop's effigy in brown Purbeck marble (now in the north presbytery aisle) belonged to his monument. During his episcopate the monks had, after 1274–5, rebuilt their refectory on a splendid scale, with bar tracery windows like those of the south transept. After his death they were prompted to elect the king's treasurer, John de Kirkeby, for whom the bishopric of Ely was one of the rewards of high

52. The eastern gable of Northwold's presbytery. The tracery of the north aisle window is later fourteenth century and the Perpendicular window in the south aisle lights Bishop West's chantry (completed 1534). The large pinnacle to the left of the gable is of 1846 and the tall spires of the aisle ends are c.1340.

office. He already held, quite improperly, a large number of lucrative clerical livings and was only a deacon until the time of his election. Kirkeby was ordained priest on 21 September 1286 and consecrated bishop at Canterbury the next day, after which, amid some disapproval, he hurried straight back to affairs of state in London. It was there that he built an impressive private chapel, now the church of St Etheldreda's, Holborn, which was left with the rest of his Holborn estate to the bishops of Ely on his death in 1290. Its remarkable windows are some of the earliest to demonstrate an English readiness to experiment with bar tracery as a network of shapes capable of indefi-

nite multiplication and fascinating variety. In its combination of large, traceried windows separated by decorative niches it is a significant forerunner to Ely's fourteenth-century Lady chapel.

The new bishop, William de Luda, was the keeper of the king's wardrobe, an important office of government. He died in 1298 and is commemorated by the wonderful tomb on the south side of the choir *(Fig. 51)*. It is a kind of miniature building with three gables, often compared with the very similar and contemporary tomb of Edmund Crouchback (died 1296) in the sanctuary at Westminster abbey. De Luda seems to have been the first bishop at Ely to have his effigy engraved in brass rather than sculpted. Only its outline remains, in the slab to which it was fixed.

It cannot be denied that the bishops were central to the architectural development of the cathedral during the late twelfth and thirteenth centuries. But it is important to bear in mind that records of their achievements at Ely survive by chance and because they paid for some of the great building projects. If similar notices of the different priors and their activities had also come down to us, the story of the last two chapters might have had a rather different tone. For example, although Northwold's contemporaries, Priors Ralph (1229–after 1235) and Walter (after 1241–59) are now shadowy figures, they and their sacrists would have had more direct involvement in the great thirteenth-century building campaign than their busy bishop.

Throughout this long period, however, documentary references to buildings are generally very scarce. As we enter the fourteenth century, the parchment account rolls of the various departments of the monastery begin to paint a detailed if incomplete picture of building work. The bishops continued to play an important role, but the most impressive figure during the first half of the fourteenth century was a sacrist of heroic stature and undeniable artistic intelligence, Alan of Walsingham.

5. TRIUMPH IN ADVERSITY:
The Fourteenth Century

The founding of a great new Lady chapel in 1321 begins a period of intense building activity at the cathedral. After the collapse of the Norman crossing tower in 1322, the construction of an extraordinary octagonal choir takes priority. The completion of the main masonry in 1328 initiates the building of the great timber vault and lantern. At the same time, the bishop pays for three bays of the surviving Norman east arm to be rebuilt in the new style and extensive repairs to the buttresses of Northwold's presbytery update the thirteenth-century exterior. A new church, for the parish of Holy Cross, is begun on the north side of the nave in 1359, and at the end of the century the west tower receives a new top.

We first hear of Alan of Walsingham in 1314 when, as a junior monk, he was asked to show Edward II the body of St Alban. This prestigious relic had been held at Ely since the eleventh century but the monks of St Albans strongly disputed its authenticity and were anxious to establish the pre-eminence of their relic. Edward, as the anointed sovereign, was able to judge on such questions and Alan, the monastery's goldsmith, was presumably required to prise open the reliquary. The king ruled in favour of St Albans and this early reversal was no doubt an instructive experience for the young monk, who was to encounter and surmount greater difficulties.

Alban, a martyr, was a more senior saint than Etheldreda, and his body had no doubt added significantly to the prestige of the church. Ely would have to manage without him, and the community had to consider how the power and significance of Etheldreda, and of the other Ely relics, might be given additional prominence to compensate for this setback. It was not long before an opportunity arose, but it came disguised as a catastrophe.

THE RISE OF ALAN OF WALSINGHAM

In 1316 John of Hotham became the new bishop and one of his first acts was a visitation of the monastery. He retired the aged and infirm Prior John of Fressingfield and put the monastery in the temporary charge of Alan of Walsingham, whom he made sub-prior. Walsingham had not necessarily been high in the monastic pecking order, but the Rule of St Benedict stipulates ability, irrespective of age or seniority, as the qualification for high office. In 1321 John of Crauden was made prior and Walsingham was given the additional post of sacrist. He became directly responsible for the care of the church and all its furnishings. He provided vestments, lights and incense. For the administration of the Sacrament his depart-ment provided the wine and wafers. The wine was made from grapes grown in the vineyard that Walsingham established on the sunny southern slope below the cathedral. The wafers were made from specially selected grain from the great barn in the sacrist's grange on St Mary's Street *(Fig. 73)*, ground in the sacristy horse mill and baked on the premises. His gold-smiths saw to the repair of the shrines and the making of any necessary items of liturgical metalwork. All routine building repairs at the church were his responsibility and, unless the bishop decided to build with his own funds, all new projects usually came under his direction. He financed these undertakings from a series of profitable estates dedicated to his office.

The new Lady chapel

Walsingham also held the post of keeper of the Lady chapel. The altar of the Blessed Virgin in the south aisle of the presbytery attracted offer-ings from pilgrims and was an especially popu-lar devotional focus for women. It became a magnet for some of the monks, who hoped to engage them in conversation. The injunctions which followed the visitation of Bishop Walpole in 1300 show that at this time women were to be found everywhere: in the cloister, the dormi-tory, the infirmary, the refectory and the monks' choir. Many of these were no doubt monks' relatives with *bona fide* reasons for their presence, but the bishop was especially con-cerned about the type of women that the monks encountered in the church. This problem was perhaps one of the reasons that led to the con-struction of a great new Lady chapel outside the boundary of the existing building, with an unusual system of segregated access (see p. **81**). More significant, however, was the intensifi-cation of the cult of the Virgin, which in the second half of the thirteenth century produced a new fashion for large separate chapels dedi-cated to her alone. Alan of Walsingham as sub-prior had laid the first stone of great new chapel on Lady Day 1321 *(Fig. 65)* and the project promised to be the all-consuming task of the next few years. The new building was laid out in five bays on the north side of the presbytery following the model of Peterborough, whose new Lady chapel had been built in 1272–90.

The fall of the Norman crossing tower

The eleventh-century choir of Abbot Simeon was still standing. Not long after the Lady chapel foundation ceremony worrying signs of instability were noticed in his crossing, where the great Norman bell tower rose above the stalls of the monks. By the following February these were so conspicuous that the monks had abandoned their choir and were worshipping in the chapel of St Catharine in the east walk of the cloisters. On 12 February 1322, just as the monks had retired to their dormitory for the night, the tower fell with a concussion that shook the town of Ely like an earthquake. The centre of the church was reduced to rubble and as the chronicler relates:

the aforesaid Sacrist Alan, vehemently grieved and earnestly sorrowful at this disastrous and lament-able event, for a moment knew not which way to turn himself or what to do for the reparation of such a ruin. But, recovering his courage, and greatly confident in the help of God and of his pious mother Mary, and also in the merits of the holy virgin Etheldreda, he laid his hand to the work; and first, with great labour and expense, he caused to be removed from within the church the stones and timber which had fallen in the ruin, and also the superabundance of dust which was there, with all possible speed to be cleared away, and having measured out by architectural art, in the place where he was about to construct the new campanile, eight positions in which the eight columns of stone supporting the whole edifice

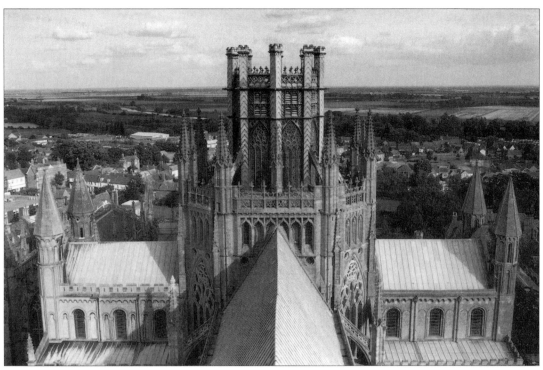

53. The octagon seen from the west tower. Most of the stonework was built between 1322 and 1328. The lead and timber lantern was complete by 1340; its external appearance today is due to Gilbert Scott's restoration of 1861–73, which relied upon the evidence of old engravings and a study of its medieval timbers. The stone pinnacle tops are also by Scott. They seem to have been left unfinished by the medieval builders.

were to be erected and beneath which the choir and its stalls was afterwards to be constructed, he caused them to be dug out and examined, till he had found a solid place where the foundation of the work could be securely begun. These aforesaid eight places, then having been solicitously proved and with stones and sand firmly consolidated, he then at last began the eight columns and the subsequent stonework, which work indeed, was completed up to the higher cornice through six years to the year of our Lord 1328.

The comprehensive character of the long passage from which this description comes suggests that it may have been derived from a memorandum by the sacrist himself. It includes a careful record of the new sacristy buildings which he built and it continues with an anguished

account of the theft and recovery of the Anglo-Saxon cross of King Edgar (see p. 8), one of the most precious treasures in his care. Its main subject is, of course, the creation of a quite extraordinary building, a huge stone octagon with a magnificent and unprecedented timber vault and lantern (*Figs. 53, 54 and Col. pl. 7*).

THE OCTAGON AND LANTERN: DESIGNERS

Walsingham is an interesting example of an informed architectural patron and it is clear that he played a leading role in the direction of the work. The extent to which he should be seen as the architect is open to discussion. The parchment account rolls of the sacrist, which survive from the second year of construction,

disclose the part played by two other individuals: Master John the mason and Master William Hurley, the king's carpenter. There are good reasons for supposing the master mason was John Ramsey and that he designed all the details of the octagon masonry and supervised its construction. The octagon and related works at Ely are created in a personal architectural language. It can also be encountered in the cloisters at Norwich, where John Ramsey is documented, and in other buildings where Alan of Walsingham can have played no part. It has, moreover, been shown by Christopher Wilson that the work of the following decade at Ely shows the hand of John Ramsey's more famous relative William, who became master of the king's works. He is mentioned in the Ely sacrist's roll for 1336–7, when he was paid for repairing old windows and also received the robe that was part of his due as master mason. He became a close professional colleague of William Hurley in important projects at Windsor and Westminster in this decade, but was one of the many victims of the Black Death of 1348–9.

FORM AND MEANING IN THE OCTAGON

The sacrist had the best professional help available for the achievement of his vision, but there can be little doubt that the basic idea was conceived in his mind and guided by him. What was that idea and why did it take such an unusual form?

It is true that English architecture around 1300 shows a new interest in polygonal shapes in castles and churches, but this alone hardly explains why a great octagon should have been introduced into the crossing of a Benedictine cathedral. The hexagonal crossing of Sienna cathedral is earlier (finished c.1260) and may

54. (left) The interior of the octagon from the north transept wall walk. (Photograph by Philip Dixon)

have influenced Arnolfo de Cambio's octagon in the cathedral at Florence (designed in 1294 and built on a larger scale after 1368). But it is more likely that both these Italian examples and Ely's octagon are ultimately derived from authoritative early Christian buildings where a centralised plan form was frequently used to mark a major burial site. The church of the Holy Sepulchre at Jerusalem is the most prestigious early example.

An interesting early northern version of this type of building is the church of St Gereon at Cologne, a largely medieval building whose oval centrepiece is a Roman Christian tomb (c.AD 400). That this association of centralised buildings with tombs endured in northern Europe is demonstrated by an impressive octagon that was begun in the late twelfth century at the east end of Trondheijm cathedral in Norway to surround the burial of St Olave.

Phillip Lindley has pointed out that Ely's octagon contained the tombs of the seven Saxon benefactors (encountered in Chapter 3), and he has argued that this was a significant factor in the choice of the centralised plan. They were buried behind the monks' stalls on the north side, which must have approximated closely to the site of their translation in 1154. Until the eighteenth century their painted images decorated the wall which backed the stallwork. Here, they might be seen and venerated by pilgrims.

The octagon sculpture

In a more general way the octagon can, of course, be interpreted as a kind of mausoleum to Etheldreda. Her life is chronicled in a series of relief sculptures *(Fig. 3)* strategically placed in the corners of the building. The fact that the shrine was further to the east is not of material significance to this grand and arcane architectural gesture. The established identifications of the individual Etheldreda reliefs should not be accepted without question. The first in the series chronologically has been wrongly identified as the 'First translation of Etheldreda' (when her body was found to be incorrupt) since James Bentham published an illustration of it in 1771. The illustration has itself been part of the problem because the artist, Theodore Heins, misrepresented the semi-naked figure on the bed in a rather androgynous fashion. It would have been quite improper in the fourteenth century to show Etheldreda naked to the waist and the details of the recumbent figure in the relief itself are better interpreted as a man, bearded and crowned. His right hand drops in the stage gesture of death while the crowned, standing figure of Etheldreda clutches his other arm in sorrow and despair. This is surely the death of her first husband, Tondberht, whom the monks firmly believed had given Etheldreda the Isle of Ely as a wedding gift. Tondberht's great gift makes him the prototype of the seven benefactors whose place of burial lay immediately below this relief.

If this is so, we have to look somewhere else for the translation which is such a vital credential of Etheldreda's sanctity. This must be the second scene in the relief on the south-west side, which has hitherto been supposed to represent, in two parts, the death of Etheldreda and the closing of her coffin before burial. It seems more likely now that the second part represents the translation of her incorrupt body into the Roman sarcophagus. The strange shape of the coffin in the relief resembles that of an unusual Roman sarcophagus of Barnack stone recently discovered at nearby Stuntney and now in the Ely museum. At the Reformation Etheldreda's coffin was revealed to be of 'common stone' rather than the marble mentioned by Bede and the *Liber Eliensis* (see pp. **5** and **102**).

On the opposite side of the south-west arch a relief shows another of Etheldreda's miracles, when in 1116 Bricstan of Chatteris was miraculously released from his prison fetters by the

55. (top) Octagon relief: Bricstan of Chatteris is released from prison. (bottom left) Octagon label stop: a queen. (bottom right) Octagon label stop: devil.

intervention of Etheldreda and St Benedict *(Fig. 55)*. The arch between these two miracle subjects begins the south aisle of the nave where, in the second bay, there appears to have been a miraculous well. Other writers have tentatively identified this place as *Crux ad Fontem* (the Cross at the Spring). This was the site of Etheldreda's original burial; the place where a spring welled forth at her first translation. The well's reputation for healing properties attracted pilgrims and offerings. The much-battered thirteenth-century arch on the outer wall between this chapel and the cloister may relate to it.

The octagon was therefore a way of drawing together a number of themes in the history of this venerable building. But it had also to function as the choir of the monks, as the immediate setting for St Benedict's *Opus Dei*. Their stalls (see p. **70**) were situated in a stone and timber enclosure at ground level and from this viewpoint, the great canopy of the lantern must have seemed to hover without visible support.

The large heads that decorate the four minor arches of the octagon peered over the top of the stalls. They represent a queen *(Fig. 55, bottom left)*, a king, a bishop, two other clergy and an apparently secular figure of no evident rank. They have been variously identified as historical figures more or less contemporary with the building of the octagon and lantern. There is, however, no evidence to identify any of them as individuals and no attempt has been made to explain the south-west arch where, in place of heads, we find a vigorous little lion and a corpulent devil armed with a circular shield or buckler *(Fig. 55, bottom right)*. So much in the octagon sculpture shows careful thought that it would be wrong to see these last two as the doodles of a craftsman who had run out of human subjects.

Next to the devil is the relief of Bricstan's shackles *(Fig. 55, top)*. Bricstan would have been recognised by the monks as a type of St Peter, whose prison chains were miraculously severed in Acts 12.7. Peter, the third dedication of the cathedral, is – as we have seen – represented as a proto-Benedictine in the presbytery vault (see p. **50**). The carved heads in fact portray a series of authority figures overlooking the choir where the Benedictine community of Ely saw itself hierarchically arrayed. Peter's first letter has instructions on leadership and humility which are not only mirrored in the Rule of St Benedict but are particularly applicable to these sculptures:

> the elders therefore among you I exhort who am a fellow elder ... tend the flock of God which is among you exercising the oversight not of constraint but willingly according unto God ...

Neither as lording it over the charge allotted to you, but making yourselves examples to the flock. And when the chief shepherd shall be manifested ye shall receive the crown of glory that fadeth not away. Likewise, ye younger, be subject unto the elder. Yea, all of you gird yourselves with humility and serve one another: for God resisteth the proud but giveth grace to the humble. Humble yourselves therefore under the mighty hand of God that he may exalt you in due time ... Be sober, be watchful; your adversary the devil as a roaring lion, walketh about, seeking whom he may devour.

> 1 Peter 5.1–8

The monks stood and sang literally under the hand of God, extended over them in the central vault boss of Christ in Judgement. The life of Etheldreda, who set aside her earthly crown in order to win 'the crown of glory that fadeth not away', was perpetually before their eyes. Did the octagon itself represent the saint's heavenly crown? This symbol was suggested by Dean Stubbs in 1897: a sentimental Victorian idea perhaps, but one that is supported by a twelfth-century Ely manuscript. This book of miracles is likely to have been used by Alan of Walsingham when he came to choose subjects for the imagery of the octagon, and in the initial which begins the life of Withburga *(Col. pl. 4, bottom right)* the early medieval hexagonal crown held by the saint makes an interesting comparison with the appearance of the octagonal lantern.

The middle zone of the octagon contains eight large empty niches and between them are twelve seated apostles by John Redfern, the Victorian sculptor. There is also a series of sixteen fine medieval heads. Their Old Testament hats meant to Redfern that they were the four major and the twelve minor prophets. This plausible suggestion justified his new apostles, who were their typological descendants. Lindley has discovered fragments of scroll-bearing figures that stood in the great niches but their identities are unclear. On the flyleaf of the twelfth-century book of miracles is a list of individuals, scribbled hastily in a four-teenth-century hand which M.R. James suggested might be 'a list of figures on a shrine or painting'. The list, which is in Latin, reads, 'Erconbert and Sexburga. Duke Tonbert. St Etheldreda. King Egfrid. St Withburga. King Wulfhere. St Ermenilda. St Peter, St Benedict.' There are ten of them and Lindley has identified two of them as the subjects of lost stained-glass windows, but this would also have been a very suitable group from which to select subjects for the eight octagon niches. Less speculation is needed to identify the tiny figures which still perch on the top of the major arches of the octagon. They are the four Evangelists and they parallel Durandus's observation that 'The church consists of four walls, that is built on the doctrine of the four Evangelists.'

57. Wells chapter house, interior (early fourteenth century).

Contemporary sources for the octagon

The mason and the carpenter had somehow to articulate the sacrist's great idea in the language of recent architectural forms. At Wells cathedral another mason with a close knowledge of fashionable royal work had recently completed a new chapter house on the customary English octagonal plan *(Figs. 56 and 57)*. It is the closest relative of the octagon in form, scale and date, although it differs in construction and purpose. Raised on a lower chamber built in the closing decades of the thirteenth century, it was completed in a second campaign, probably before 1307.

There are three points of unusual correspondence with Ely. Most obvious is the little continuous gallery that runs round the top of both buildings. Then there is the design of the buttresses which, at ground level – and excep-

56. Wells chapter house (early fourteenth century).

tionally at this date – present an angle rather than a flat face. Finally, and less obviously, there is the vault which at Wells represents the application of a tierceron scheme (such as the one used over Northwold's presbytery) to an octagonal plan. The great stone span of Wells requires a central column. But if this column and the cone of ribs which it supports are mentally eliminated, what remains is exactly the pattern of the timber vault at Ely, with all its ribs and bosses.

Technical challenges: the vault and lantern

The Ely octagon was cut into the crossing of a major Romanesque church and we need to remember that it was not intended to create the great open circulation space which we see today.

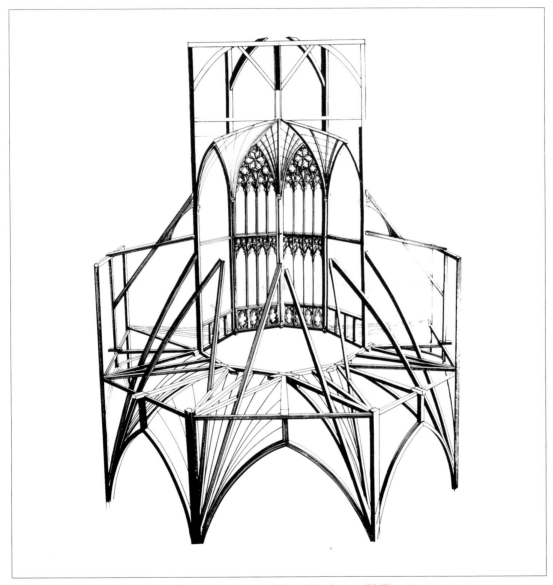

58. Cecil Hewett's reconstruction of the octagon carpentry in its original state. (Phillimore)

Because the stalls of the monks ran through the centre, a central column was not an option. Given the enormous span, there can never have been any serious question of a stone vault. Timber vaulting, in imitation of stone, had been a distinctive feature of English architecture since the middle of the thirteenth century but none had presented the technical challenge offered by the octagon. The chronicle suggests that the stonework was completed in 1328 and the construction of the timberwork, by William Hurley, probably began shortly afterwards. The great lower vault was being painted in 1334–5 and the building was completed in 1339–40, when John of Burwell carved the boss of Christ in Majesty and the lantern windows were glazed.

The carpentry structure was much altered in the eighteenth century but the medieval scheme was reconstructed by Cecil Hewett in 1985 *(Fig. 58)* and is to be the subject of a detailed analysis by Gavin Simpson. The sacrist was active in the search for timber and chose eight of the largest trees from Chicksands in Bedfordshire. The great timbers were manipulated by cranes, probably built on the flat tops of the stone turrets of the octagon (the pinnacles were added only in the nineteenth century). Meticulous planning in which each timber was linked by clearly visible assembly marks and numbers to its companions ensured orderly construction, beginning on the east side and working clockwise. From great corner posts fixed into prepared masonry slots in the corners of the stone octagon, triangulated brackets were assembled and joined into an octagonal ring of short timbers which forms the base of the lantern. Raking timbers of exceptional length rise from the base of the corners to support the vertical posts of the lantern. These posts are in two sections, joining at the base of the lantern windows where there is iron reinforcement. The longer, upper posts form the sides of both the lantern and the belfry above. (Six bells, two of which may now survive in the west tower, were

rung by ropes which passed through the upper vault of the lantern down to the floor on the south side of the octagon.) The whole timber structure is clad externally in lead.

The stalls

The lantern is carpentry on a heroic scale but it seems clear that William Hurley was also responsible for the miniature delicacy of the elegant stalls *(Fig. 59)*, which lay beneath this mighty canopy. The resident carpenter at Ely from 1336 to 1350 was Master Geoffrey de Middylton and he would doubtless have carried out much of the work which the busy Hurley devised. Walsingham, for his part, delegated the organisation of work on the stalls to another monk, Brother R. of Saxmundham. The forty-six medieval stalls that stand today in the western bays of the presbytery are the survivors of a group of seventy begun in 1338 and finished by 1348. Kate Fearn's recent research has shown that although they are now of uniform design, the seats of the bishop and prior, which would have terminated the western end of each side, had slightly richer canopies than the rest. The stalls replaced a thirteenth-century set of which small fragments survive. All the stalls had misericords, carved brackets which appear when the seats are tipped up and upon which the monks could rest their posteriors when the liturgy required them to stand for long periods. There are relatively few conventional religious subjects among the misericords: a miracle of St Giles, the beheading of John the Baptist and an unusual image of Noah. His ark *(Fig. 60)* makes detailed reference to the architecture of the

59. (right) The stalls (1338–48). The rectilinear framework makes a striking contrast with the luxuriant curving forms of the octagon and Lady chapel tabernacles of more than a decade earlier. The carved reliefs of 1851–65 are mainly by M. Abeloos of Louvain.

60. Misericord: Noah's ark rendered in the architectural language of the octagon.

61. Misericord: a bear shakes apes out of a tree while hares crouch in the undergrowth. Monkeys and hares were emblems of lust in the Middle Ages, but according to the Bestiary the bear could symbolise Christian conversion. The cubs were thought to be born formless and were literally licked into shape by their mother.

octagon in its curving castellated gunwales and turreted superstructure. Many more are emblematic of the sins of the flesh, particularly lust, against which the monks of Ely must strive in order to win their heavenly crowns *(Fig. 61)*. The carving throughout is excellent.

BISHOP HOTHAM'S CHOIR BAYS

The monastic chronicler relates that in spite of the collapse of the tower, miraculously no harm had come to the 'great and beautiful fabric which rises above the tomb of the holy Virgin' (Northwold's presbytery) thanks to the protection of God and the merits of Etheldreda. Certainly, the Norman choir had been damaged at its western end. Once the octagon was conceived, there was every reason to think about the remodelling of the three surviving Romanesque bays that housed the altar of the monks' choir. Here was an opportunity for Bishop Hotham to extend the work of Bishop Northwold and this he did at considerable personal expense. The work of the octagon, financed by the sacrist's department and a series of donations, had cost £2,400 6s 11d. Hotham's new choir bays were almost as expensive and came out at £2,034 12s 8³/₄d. They are thought to have been finished by the time of the bishop's death in 1337.

Admirers of Bishop Northwold's work *(Col. pl. 5)* sometimes deride Hotham's bays *(Fig. 62)* as fussy and ornate, whereas they should revere them for their subtle and decorous response to the peerless grandeur of the thirteenth-century architecture. The balance of materials, Barnack and Purbeck marble, is strictly governed by the old work but everywhere the weighty opulence of Northwold is transformed into a crisp and elegant essay in tracery design. The windows and gallery openings are marvellous examples of the sinuous curvilinear tracery which was one of the significant contributions of English masons to the development of gothic. Here stone appears to achieve the ductile qualities of metal. Certainly, there is no need to labour the comparison between the fourteenth-century work at Ely and the magnificent contemporary censer and incense boat of Ramsey abbey, which were fished out of the fen in 1850 *(Fig. 64)*.

The masons John and William Ramsey must clearly have been connected in some way with

62. (right) The richly decorated southern elevation of Bishop Hotham's choir of c.1322–37. The right-hand bay of the arcade and tribune represents the first phase of the design. (National Monuments Record)

63. The vault of Bishop Hotham's choir continues the theme of Northwold's presbytery vault, adding extra tierceron and lierne ribs to make a more complex pattern. It respects the important symbolism of the earlier vault sculpture by avoiding figure subjects and using exclusively foliage bosses. (National Monuments Record)

Ely's great Benedictine neighbour. Successive contributions to the architecture of Hotham's choir are plain to see once they have been pointed out. The aisles are complicated. But of the two main internal elevations it seems that John Ramsey probably built the three arches of the south side, the western bay of the gallery and the eastern and western windows of the south clerestory. William appears to have built the middle and eastern bay of the gallery, and the central window of the clerestory. If this sequence appears to defy structural logic, we have to remember that this elevation was probably gradually remodelled out of the standing

Norman work rather than rebuilt from the ground. William Ramsey can also be credited with the whole of the northern elevation.

A striking feature of this work, for all its curvaceous tracery detail, is the dominance of rectangular forms in the framing of the lower and middle storeys. The same tendency can be seen in the stall canopies. It is very much part of the vocabulary of William Ramsey who, in other buildings, is recognised as a founding father of the Perpendicular style whose controlling rectangles and dominant verticals were to characterise English architecture until the Reformation.

Hotham chose the site of his burial, in the central bay, in a rather distinctive fashion. He was returning to the vestry, the chronicler tells us, having celebrated mass at the high altar, when his pastoral staff broke (croziers were often made in demountable sections for ease of transport). Hotham paused and pronounced that this spot would be the place of his tomb. He then told John of Crauden, who would have been immediately ahead of him in the procession, that the prior would be buried at the bishop's feet.

The incident is another striking example of the medieval awareness of history and precedent that is so much a part of the cathedral's architecture and imagery. The *Liber Eliensis* describes how one of the seven benefactors, Wulfstan, archbishop of York, chose the original site of his tomb. He had probably been an Ely monk in the early eleventh century and, late in life, during a visit to the abbey, he entered the church in procession with the monks. At a certain point they halted. The aged Wulfstan leant on his staff which, finding a fissure in the pavement, sank up to half its length. This, declared the archbishop, would be the place where his body would lie.

Hotham suffered a paralysing stroke in 1334, when his new choir bays were only half built and died three years later. His tomb, which was

64. The censer and incense boat of Ramsey abbey (c.1325). Silver-gilt, silver and parcel-gilt. (Victoria & Albert Museum)

moved to the south side of the presbytery in the eighteenth century, was originally surmounted by an effigy of the bishop in alabaster. He had also commissioned for the monks' choir a great seven-branched candlestick which must have been one of the wonders of its age. It was decorated with images of the Creation and the Fall of Man, four figures of kings in arms and four dragons. Following Hotham's death the monks elected John of Crauden, but this was frustrated by Pope Benedict XII, who translated Simon Montacute from Worcester.

THE LADY CHAPEL

Bishop Montacute, who was enthroned in 1337 and died in 1344, is closely associated with the building of the Lady chapel *(Fig. 65)*. But what had been achieved between the false start of 1321 and his arrival? From the beginning, the administration of the Lady chapel project was delegated to Brother John of Wisbech, who saw it more or less complete by the time of his death in 1349. In the latter stages he had a good deal of help. Montacute evidently gave generously to

the project after 1337 and Crauden left £100 in his will in 1341. The early years of the project must have been difficult with so much of the sacrist's resources swallowed up by the octagon. The chronicler states quite clearly that at one point there was not enough money to pay the workmen and relates the miraculous discovery of a coin hoard in an earthenware pot discovered on the site of the chapel. John of Wisbech hid the treasure under his bed in the dormitory, rubbed the coins clean with water and lime and paid the workmen.

It is not clear when this happened. The earliest phase of the chapel was probably extremely expensive, involving as it did the construction of arguably the most elaborate wall arcade yet built in Europe *(Figs. 65 and 83)*. It contains a series of double seats. Over each pair, supported by buttresses of Purbeck marble, are arches with three-dimensional double curves known as nodding ogees (seen also in the octagon niches). Everything in this design is in movement and every surface of the soft clunch is carved in minute detail. This kind of architecture was normally reserved for small and costly furnishings and for the bases of shrines. In a sense, however, the Lady chapel was conceived as a great shrine to the Virgin. The story of her life and miracles, derived from apocryphal accounts, is told in detail in beautiful relief sculpture between the arcade canopies. The hammers of the iconoclasts have hampered the task of identification but the themes were first unravelled in 1892 by M.R. James, whose well-known ghost stories were an offshoot of his formidable scholarship in medieval studies.

It was suggested by Canon Stewart that the elegant curve of the Lady chapel stall backs was inspired by the thirteenth-century niches of the Galilee porch *(Fig. 47)*. One of the themes of the fourteenth-century work at Ely is indeed the interest which it shows in the earlier architecture of the cathedral. In Hotham's choir this is obvious and even in the octagon there are

attempts to make visual associations between new and old decorative detail. The bull's eye windows (seen also in the octagon and lantern) that ventilate the space above the Lady chapel vaults were therefore no doubt inspired by those on the twelfth-century west tower. Christopher Wilson's assertion that octagon, choir and Lady chapel and Prior Crauden's chapel were all begun by one mason is supported by this evidence of a pervasive respect for the old work.

Prior Crauden built his remarkable chapel in 1324–5 *(Fig. 66)*. The curved window jambs here are a novelty in fourteenth-century architecture, but they were probably derived from a study of the Galilee niches. The exquisite carving of the tabernacles is close in feeling to the Lady chapel wall arcades and suggests that they could have been completed in the late 1320s. The glorious superstructure of the Lady chapel was largely complete by 1349, the year in which John of Wisbech and half the Ely monks died in the Black Death, and the altar was dedicated by Bishop de Lisle in 1352–3. There is, however, some doubt about the vault, which joins very awkwardly (see p. **97**). The great side walls of the Lady chapel with their handsome windows must have risen slowly in the early 1330s but the two gable ends cannot have been tackled much before the end of the decade. Phillip Lindley has identified shields bearing the arms of Bishop Montacute about a third of the way up the chapel's west front which show that this part could not have been reached before his arrival in 1337.

65. (left) Lady chapel interior (1321–53). The complex and beautiful walls of the Lady chapel had probably been planned by Master John from the outset and are closely related to design ideas in the octagon and Prior Crauden's chapel. The digging of its foundations in 1321 may have affected the ground drainage beneath the church and caused the fall of the crossing tower in 1322. (National Monuments Record)

The west front *(Fig. 12)* is the principal façade of the building and is completely covered by statue niches and heraldry. Our view of it today differs substantially from its original context in which it would have been concealed from long views by the vanished northern arm of the west front. Its rich decoration must be one of the main reasons for believing that the doorway in the west aisle of the north transept was, in its original state, the main entrance for pilgrims. But it is the interior of the chapel that creates the greatest impact. Ways of combining sculpture and wall shafts, evolved in Prior Crauden's chapel and the niches of the octagon, find their full expression in these remarkable walls. The vault is visually supported by shafts which begin their ascent behind the dado arcades and continue upwards underneath double tiers of statue niches, creating an exhilarating interplay of structural and decorative members. A building of such complexity had never been seen before and in its heyday it was alive with images. Even the monastic chronicler thought the amount of sculpture remarkable. He carefully recorded a grand total of 'one hundred and forty-seven images inside and outside the chapel besides the tiny images above the altar and the figures in the doorway at the entrance to the chapel'. When the pilgrims entered and took their seats in the wall arcade they became part of a great company of the heavenly host. The architecture and sculpture of the eastern bays were richly coloured *(Col. pl. 9)* and the windows contained sumptuous stained glass *(Col. pl. 8)* of which a substantial fragment has been reassembled on the south side.

It is well worth studying the extensive traces of colour on the masonry and considering the important part that paint once played in the fourteenth-century architecture at Ely. Victorian watercolour reconstructions by the architect William Burges indicate the lavish livery of Prior Crauden's chapel and similar colours can be seen in their faded state on some of the

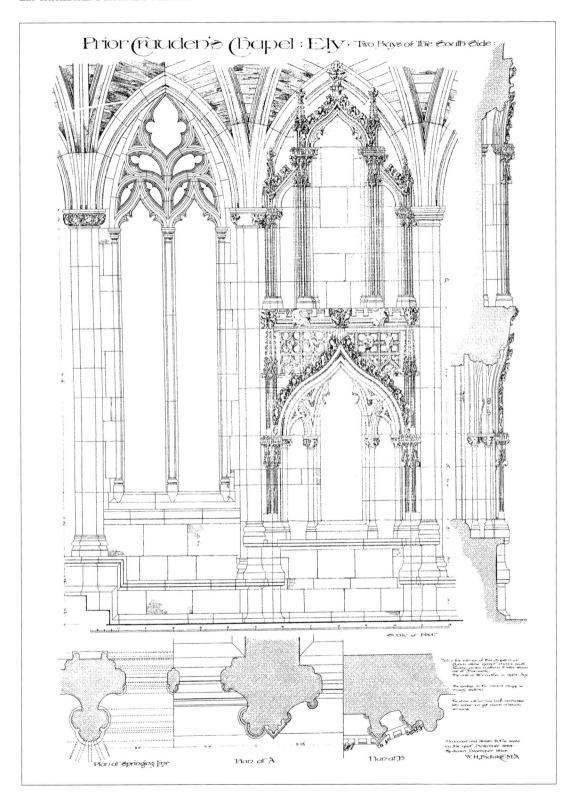

Prior Crauden's Chapel : Ely · Two Bays of the South Side :

Scale of Feet.

Plan at Springing line

Plan at A

Plan at B

W. H. Bidlake M.A

contemporary stone presbytery furnishings. In the north-east corner of the Lady chapel vault one can make out the remains of a scheme of painted tracery which, if it was completed, would have added considerably to the complexity of its already ornate lierne vault. Early photographs and engravings show that the vault webs of the octagon were once similarly decorated with tracery forms.

The parish church of Holy Cross

As these great works of the first half of the fourteenth century came to a close the monks turned their attention to other projects. In 1315 a canon of Wells had undertaken a visitation on behalf of the archbishop of Canterbury. He was critical of the confusion created by the parish services at the nave altar. Not altogether surprisingly, these were plainly audible in the monks' choir. Stone for the foundations of a new parish church was purchased in 1342 but it was not until 1359 that work began on a new building attached to the north aisle of the nave. The sacrist's roll for the period records in detail the ordering of cut stone in varied shapes as well as timber, iron and glass. This work may be associated with a large payment in the same year for demolishing and removing stone, timber and thatch at the 'Trasor', which was perhaps a large mason's workshop then occupying the site of the new church. The new building, in recognition of the former site before the nave altar, was dedicated as the church of Holy Cross by Bishop Simon Langham (1362–6).

66. (left) Prior Crauden's chapel (1324–5) was probably designed by Master John, the mason whose fertile imagination gave birth to the octagon, Lady chapel and Hotham's choir bays. W.H. Bidlake's drawing, made in 1884 shows one wall of the prior's chapel and illustrates this great medieval architect's brilliant command of three-dimensional geometry.

The western octagon

When was Bishop Northwold's great spire removed from the west tower and replaced by the present western octagon? *(Fig. 22)* The traceried windows of the new top are the best indication of its date. They closely resemble the tracery in the east window of Witchford church, near Ely, which is associated with a reconsecration of 1376. John Harvey, however, conjectures that the western octagon was in fact the 'new work' started in 1392–3 when Master Robert was given a special gift of 6s 4d. This was Robert Wodehirst, a distinguished Norwich mason, who was working at Ely from 1387 to 1393 on the building of a new high altar reredos.

As we have seen, the western octagon sits on the thick masonry base of what may have been a substantial predecessor. The walls of the west tower, including the wall passage, are about 3 metres thick. Even the outer leaf is 1–5 metres thick. And yet the walls of the western octagon are a mere 50 centimetres in thickness and are now stabilised by an elaborate internal carpentry spider. Externally it is braced by four turrets whose panelled faces are copied from the main octagon pinnacles. In spite of its bold silhouette, this is a relatively light, almost flimsy structure. This building is often blamed for the structural problems of the west tower, but it is possible that it was an early attempt to reduce the weight of stone, lead and timber bearing down on the ancient tower. Until the late eighteenth century it had a little timber spire which rose from behind its battlements like the spirelets common among the parish churches of Hertfordshire *(Fig. 86)*.

Remodelling Northwold's choir

The fourteenth-century work at Ely is so beautiful that it is easy to forget that much of it was associated with the mundane business of correcting earlier structural failure. This was evidently

67. The south side of the choir. The central bays preserve the external tribune openings and flying buttresses of Northwold's presbytery. On either side are the traceried windows of at least two fourteenth-century remodelling campaigns. Hotham's work is on the left.

the reason for the major mid-fourteenth-century campaign in which the upper parts of the buttresses of Bishop Northwold's presbytery were mainly replaced. If one stands at one end of the south aisle it is very clear that the thirteenth-century walls lean outwards at a considerable angle. The divergence between the aisle buttresses and the main elevation is magnified at the top of the building, where the delicate upper arches of Northwold's elegant, double flying buttresses are likely to have collapsed. Even those that survive today show signs of distress. The fourteenth-century masons took the opportunity to introduce a more efficient system of abutment and to build a series of strikingly elegant traceried windows

to light the thirteenth-century galleries *(Figs. 43 and 67)*. They are all but identical to the closely contemporary cloister windows of the church of La Chaise Dieu in the Massif Central begun in 1343 as the mausoleum of Pope Clement VI. Jean Bony has already pointed out that details similar to those in Prior Crauden's chapel and Mildenhall church are to be seen in the tomb of Abbot Renaud of La Chaise Dieu, who died in 1346. The work undertaken at Ely in these years stands comparison with anything on the continent and we should perhaps not be surprised if it was emulated in work produced by this remarkably cosmopolitan papal court.

PILGRIMS, SHRINES AND LITURGICAL FITTINGS

The arrangement of the Norman church was complicated by the additions of later periods, but the allocation of space remained broadly the same throughout the Middle Ages. It is well worth studying carefully the plan of 1742 published by Browne Willis (see Plan 2). This predates the great mid-eighteenth-century reordering and shows several of the medieval internal divisions before their destruction in 1770–1.

In the earlier period we have discerned some liturgical change, but in the later medieval phases the most dynamic element was associated with shrines and pilgrimage. Pilgrims were a significant source of revenue and, as we have seen, the architectural expression of the church as the shrine of Etheldreda had a powerful influence on new projects. Most of the relics and sites of interest were east of the crossing. The building of Northwold's presbytery created a large area for Etheldreda and the other saints. The monks' choir would have been completely private with its own altar backed by a screen and flanked by paired entrances. These led to the high altar sanctuary, which seems to have taken up the two eastern bays of Hotham's work and one of Northwold's. The high altar's late four-teenth-century reredos would have been a sub-stantial and richly ornamented division. Beyond it lay the shrine, in its own enclosure, with an altar at its western end. Sitting on a tall, marble base, the glittering reliquary ornamented with silver figures and studded with jewels may have been visible above the high altar reredos. The timber screens of separate chapels would have divided the presbytery aisles. There were evi-

68. This mysterious structure, which could have been the base of a shrine, was built during the campaign that completed Hotham's choir in the late 1330s. It retains much original colour and is decorated with the heads of monks and of a bishop. Beneath it are grouped some fragments of the thirteenth-century shrine base of Etheldreda.

dently three altars in the north presbytery aisle alone, and next to the monument of Bishop Gunning in the south aisle one can still see the double piscina basins of the former Lady chapel altar, where the sacred vessels were washed.

The shrines were cleared away in the late 1530s but pieces of their masonry platforms remain. Most impressive is the richly decorated box-like structure (Fig. 68), which stands on open arcades in the north choir aisle. It does not resemble the typical English shrine base where the lower part is usually expressed as niches in solid masonry. It is much more like certain Italian shrines where the reliquary stands on pillars that allow the faithful to get right under the saint's body. Influence from Italy has been detected in contemporary wall paintings at Ely (see p. 88). What relic it housed is not known, but Withburga is a possibility.

Secondary attractions were provided by the high altar and the altar of the relics. On one of the northern pillars of the presbytery hung the shackles from which Bricstan had been miracu-lously released by the intervention of Etheldreda and Benedict. Miniature replicas, called 'Audrey's chains', could be bought by pilgrims along with other souvenirs associated with Etheldreda, including a special kind of lace. Ely's cheap pilgrim ephemera gave the English language the word 'tawdry'.

By the fourteenth century, if not earlier, it appears that the pilgrims' entrance was through a door in the west aisle of the north transept. From here they made their way up the north choir aisle to the thirteenth-century presbytery where they could circulate reasonably freely. The new Lady chapel would have been a high point of the visit and a recent archaeological study by Philip Dixon and John Heward has suggested that monks and pilgrims were care-fully separated by a system of dual access routes. The pilgrims passed through a splendid arch-way in the north presbytery aisle, beneath a seated figure of the Virgin, and via a passage to

69. This screen fragment of c.1340 may be part of the rood screen which stood in the nave before the pulpitum.

the double doorway in the centre of the Lady chapel south wall. The impressive tiled floor of this former thoroughfare now lies in the south transept.

This passage would no doubt also have been used for processions by the monks on special days. But the everyday route for monks celebrating at the Lady chapel altar was via a bridge across the north aisle. This led through an external door to a raised covered walk in front of the north transept windows. Where it met the Lady chapel this smaller passage turned right and pierced the buttresses. As it approached the eastern bays, it descended in a staircase to the chapel's sanctuary door. It is not clear how the monks ascended to the bridge from their choir (unless one of the two staircases of the pulpitum led to a raised walk behind the stalls). The interior of the chapel would have been divided by screens, so there would have been no opportunity for the monks to make conversation with the women who came to give offerings to the Virgin (see p. **62**). Most monks in fact had very little reason to be in the chapel as the services here were usually sung by a choir of boys.

In the south aisle of the nave was perhaps the site of Etheldreda's first burial, *Crux ad Fontem*, and next to it the altar of the Holy Cross, where substantial offerings were made. The altar was backed by the pulpitum and its sanctuary was defined by a timber rood screen of the type found in parish churches. There are many marks and iron attachments on the piers around this site which were connected with the rood beams, lights, hangings and other paraphernalia surrounding the sculpture group of the Crucifixion which gave this place its name, 'The Black Rood'. The closed-up sockets on the piers corresponding to the position of the rood screen exactly fit the horizontal members of the handsome timber screen that now encloses the chapel of St Edmund (*Fig. 69*). This is much-repaired carpentry of the late 1330s and the tracery is copied from Hotham's clerestory. The off-centre entrance shows that it belonged to something much wider. If the bay module is multiplied, it fits the width of the nave.

6. The Monastery

'We propose, therefore to establish a school of the Lord's service, and in setting it up we shall lay down nothing that is harsh or hard to bear ... through the continual practice of monastic observance and the life of faith, our hearts are opened wide, and the way of God's commandments is run in a sweetness of love that is beyond words. Let us then never withdraw from discipleship to him, but persevering in his teachings in the monastery until death, let us share the suffering of Christ through patience, and so deserve also a share in his kingdom.'

From the prologue to the Rule of St Benedict

The monks of Ely had, since the time of Æthelwold and Dunstan in the tenth century, followed the sixth-century Rule of St Benedict. It required the abandonment of personal property together with vows of chastity and obedience as the prerequisites for a communal life of prayer and work. Foremost was the *Opus Dei*, the observance of the seven offices which would take four or five hours out of the average day and perhaps eight on Sunday. The remaining hours were for administrative or physical work and reading. The monks were well provided for and their life was no harder than that of their secular contemporaries. They could expect a decent period of uninterrupted sleep before the night office and their diet was more than adequate. After the Conquest the church and monastery at Ely were gradually redeveloped on a typical Benedictine plan, in which a square cloister south of the church gave access to the key buildings, including dormitory, refectory and chapter house.

The monastic community

The monastery was led by an abbot until the establishment of the bishopric in 1109. Nominally, the bishop retained the role of abbot but that was exercised only through occasional formal visitations. The community can rarely have reached the total of seventy-two monks recorded in 1093. There were thirty-one monks in 1229 and from the fourteenth to the early sixteenth century the numbers ranged between the upper forties to the low thirties.

After 1109 the monastery was governed by a prior. He delegated responsibility to a group of around seventeen senior monks called 'obedientiaries' who raised income for their work from designated manors and farms. The sacrist, the treasurer, the almoner, the cellarer and the infirmarer were the most powerful of these. They and the prior ran individual households and in so doing departed from the ideal of communal life embodied in the Rule. The obedientiaries probably employed around sixty servants and recent research on monastic communities suggests that these stipendiary servants would have employed their own labour. Finally, we have to add a significant population of chaplains, chantry priests and singing boys as well as resident poor men to get a full picture of the medieval community. Its scale and complexity is commemorated today by a remarkable collection of medieval buildings.

The Rule taught that Christ was to be met in other people and for this reason hospitality was central to Benedictine life. It was carefully structured at Ely according to social status. Those with enough horses in their retinues would be entertained in the prior's house. Others went to a series of hostelries, some of whose positions have yet to be established.

THE MONASTIC BUILDINGS

Individual buildings were rebuilt, altered or extended until by the time the monastery was suppressed in the Dissolution of 1539 it had become the great complex shown in the plan *(Fig. 70)*. The uses assigned to the various buildings are those recorded in Henry VIII's award of 1541, which distributed the former accommodation of the monks among the dean and chapter of the newly constituted secular cathedral. Most of the uses will have attached to these sites since the twelfth century. In the centuries after the Reformation some buildings were demolished and others adapted in a variety of ways.

The **cloister** is the core of the monastic complex. The remaining sections are a rebuilding of 1509–10, and represent a slight enlargement of the original twelfth-century plan. This was the most important circulation route in the monastery and was also used by the majority of monks for study. Here was the monastic library which at the time of Ranulf Flambard's inventory following the death of Abbot Simeon in 1093 contained 208 volumes of which it is

thought only 30 or 40 would have been added by the Normans to the pre-Conquest library. Details of subsequent additions in the collection are sparse but among the small handful of books mentioned by Leyland in 1536–40 was a copy of Aldhelm's treatise on virginity (see **p. 4**). The precentor was responsible for the collection and for keeping a record of all books borrowed by the monks.

The **chapter house** (demolished after the Reformation) was used for meetings of the monastic community. Here a chapter of the Rule of St Benedict was read out each day, decisions were taken and discipline was administered. It was separated from the south transept of the cathedral by a vaulted corridor sometimes called a slype (and shown by Atkinson as the chapel of St Catharine) which led from the cloister to the monks' burial ground. Its early thirteenth-century capitals still adhere to the south transept.

The **dormitory** (demolished) was a first-floor building running over the top of the chapter house. It butted against the south wall of the transept, where the scar may still be seen. All the ordinary monks slept here in cubicles beneath a thatched roof. They were allowed to read in bed, and it was here that they would have kept the items of clothing and equipment allotted to them under the Rule. These included bedding, their black habits (furred and plain), underclothes, socks, shaving tackle, a dirty clothes bag, a silver spoon, a bedside mug, needle and thread, writing equipment and other items. These are set out in a list for Ely novices which is preserved in the library at Lambeth Palace. South of the chapter house the dormitory was supported by a vaulted undercroft, one bay of which survives.

This formed the link between the main cloister and the **dark cloister** *(Fig. 71)*, which was added in the thirteenth century to provide covered access to the infirmary. Its lower windows were shuttered in winter months and

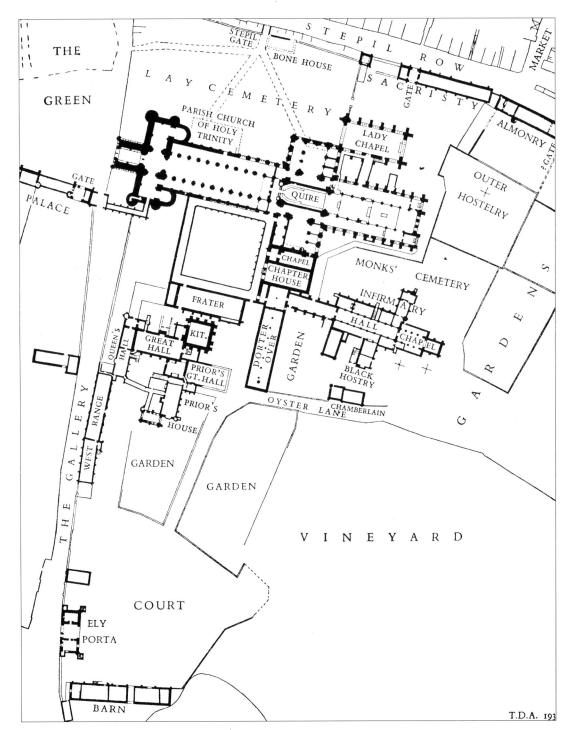

70. Plan of the monastery. (T.D. Atkinson, Victoria County History)

only a little light would have penetrated through the small oculi above; hence the name. There was a song school above this passage in 1541.

The **infirmary** *(Fig. 33)* was probably built between 1170 and 1180 and has been the subject of a recent study by Anne Holton-Krayenbuhl. It would have been visited by the monks in periods of sickness and for routine blood-letting and was also the place where most members of the community could expect to spend their last days. It is therefore a building of dignity and great quality. The nine-bay aisled hall is attached to a handsome chapel in the same style with a rib-vaulted sanctuary *(Fig. 34)*. In this chapel the bodies of the monks would rest overnight before a funeral in the cathedral. The lodging of the sub-prior once lay to the south of the chapel, next to the blood-letting hall, but in 1334, Alan of Walsingham (sub-prior and sacrist) built a new house which took up the eastern part of the north aisle. It includes a first-floor hall called the Painted Chamber. He had a life interest in the building, which was also intended for the occasional entertainment of the monks' female relatives whose presence in other parts of the monastery was frowned upon in Bishop Walpole's visitations. Two more lodgings, perhaps for the comfort of sick monks, were added to the west at about the same time, completing the annexation of the north aisle. The south aisle also was eventually subdivided into separate chambers.

The **Black Hostelry** was built onto the south side of the infirmary in the late thirteenth century as lodgings for visiting Benedictines and was named after the colour of their habits. Finally, in the sixteenth century the central space of the infirmary hall was unroofed so that

71. (left) The south transept and octagon rise above the wall of the dark cloister (c.1230), whose windows are now blocked.

a handsome new second-floor chamber on the north side could receive light through the former clerestory windows, reversing their original use. In the early days the infirmary was one of the few places where a fire was kept, and its kitchen continued to supply meat at times when the Rule banned it from the refectory menu. These comforts attracted the extra domestic establishments described above so that, as Barbara Harvey has written of the Westminster infirmary, 'At times the sick had a struggle to keep a foothold here.'

To the south of the infirmary lay the **cellarer's building** (now incorporated in Canonry House) and on the south side of the infirmary garden (well stocked with medicinal herbs) was the **chamberlain's building**. The cellarer had overall responsibility for the supply of food within the monastery and the chamberlain looked after clothing and ran the bath house. Somewhere in this area was the establishment of the pittancer, who supplemented the normal diet of the monks in the refectory with allowances of extra food on special days.

The **refectory** (or **frater**) lay to the south of the cloister but only one wall now remains. Money was being collected for a new refectory in 1274–5. Silence was kept during meals, according to the Rule, so that the monks could attend to readings. They communicated at table by a sign language which is specified in an Ely manuscript. At meals great quantities of beer were allowed. Basic dishes, or 'generals', were supplemented with 'pittances' on designated days.

The **kitchen** in 1541 was the square building of which two walls survive on the south side of the refectory. This is an imposing structure of the late twelfth century whose plan, nine square bays vaulted on four columns, attenuated proportions and elegant detailing would not have disgraced an apartment of higher status. There were other kitchens at the prior's hospice, the hostelry, sacristy, infirmary and almonry.

72. *The great hall seen from the west tower. It incorporates two walls of the ruined monastic kitchen to the left. Behind the hall is the prior's hall and to the left the roof of the long, west range running down to the Porta.*

Injunctions following the visitation of Bishop Arundel in 1376 tried to concentrate catering for the refectory, prior's hospice and guests in one place.

The **prior's house** is an area where the domestic planning is dense and difficult to disentangle. It reflects the prior's obligation to provide hospitality for important guests. The earliest part is late twelfth century and has a fine undercroft. This supports the prior's small hall above. The hall was remodelled in the fourteenth century, and again in the sixteenth century, when the large square-headed windows of the east front were introduced. The new roof of the hall has been dated by its tree rings to 1524–5. North of this was the prior's kitchen

adjoining the site of the **prior's great hall**, which was demolished at the Reformation. **Prior Crauden's chapel**, a wonderfully ornate miniature oratory *(Fig. 66)*, was built by Prior John of Crauden in 1324–5. It has a remarkable mosaic floor made by a group of itinerant fourteenth-century tile makers whose work can be seen as far afield as Warden abbey in Bedfordshire and Norton priory in Cheshire. The remains of ambitious wall paintings display a sophisticated grasp of early fourteenth-century Italian art. At the same time he remodelled the adjoining hall and built a study whose timber traceried window is now in the south porch of the cathedral. First-floor walkways once linked the chapel, the study, the prior's hall and the Queen's Hall.

The **Queen's Hall** was evidently guest accommodation and its name originates in the thirteenth century. The present hall is mid-fourteenth century and is one of the buildings in which brick makes an early appearance at Ely. It has become associated popularly with the visits of Edward III's queen, Phillippa of Hainault, who was a close friend of Prior Crauden.

The **great hall** or **guest hall** *(Fig. 72)* is a much-altered building which embodies the remains of a thirteenth-century great hall whose details are closely comparable to the presbytery of Bishop Northwold. Matthew Paris records that he built a great hall and treasury at his palace at Ely. The bishop's palace (see p. **91**) is usually thought to have been on the opposite side of the modern street called the Gallery, but it is not impossible that this hall was once part of it as we do not know exactly how Abbot Hervey delineated his quarters from the monastery when he became the first bishop in 1109. The first-floor hall, built over a splendid undercroft, was extensively remodelled and added to in the fourteenth

73. *(right) The great thirteenth-century barn of the sacrist's grange (drawn by Robert Willis before its demolition in 1843).*

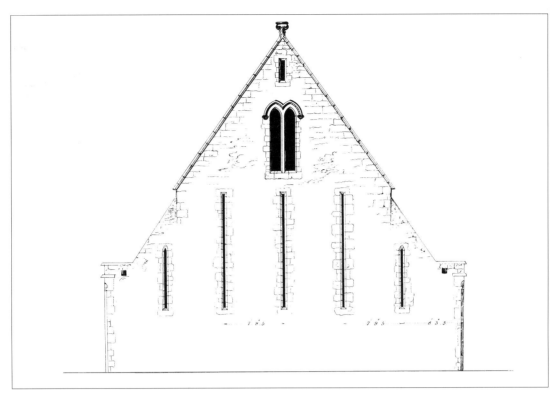

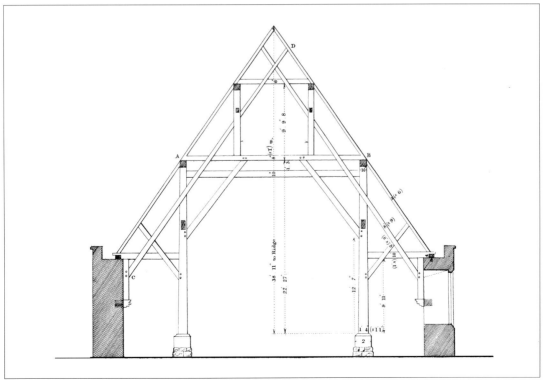

century, and was later given a new roof. Some details of this later work resemble those of the octagon. The massive additional buttresses of its southern wall were necessitated by structural movement comparable with that which afflicted the south aisle of the thirteenth-century presbytery in the century following its building.

The **west range** has the remains of a substantial late twelfth-century hall at its north end with an extremely rare contemporary roof. The whole range was altered substantially in the fourteenth and fifteenth centuries when vaulted undercrofts were introduced. Its use is not certain but guest accommodation is a possibility.

The **sacristy** was the centre of much activity. The origins of the building are ancient but much of the present structure is a rebuilding by Alan of Walsingham beginning in 1322. It is elaborately described in the monastic chronicle. The sacrist's chequer, with its chequered table for calculating, was on the first floor and beneath it was a double chamber divided by a wall which housed the goldsmiths' workshop and a cellar for the eucharistic wine. Other rooms had cupboards for other 'various necessaries of services' as well as a kitchen and a bakery, a horse mill and a larder (all used for making the eucharistic bread). The yards entered by the High Street gateway were probably used for the assembly of building materials and for workshops. A large number of varied fragments of stained glass, some of it twelfth century, have been found here, indicating an early glaziers' workshop. The **goldsmith's tower** at the west end was later adapted as the belfry of the parish of Holy Trinity who worshipped in the Lady chapel after the Reformation. The sacrist's grange on St Mary's Street had until 1843 a great barn 67 metres in length *(Fig. 73)* (see p. **124**).

Charitable giving was central to the Rule of St Benedict and the **almonry** was sited near the Market Place for the efficient delivery of alms to

74. The roof of the monastic barn (c.1400).

the deserving poor of Ely. Much of the alms consisted of very large quantities of surplus food from the refectory, produced deliberately for this purpose, so that the monks were in effect sharing their meals with the poor. The building had a chapel dedicated to St Martin, the Roman soldier who gave half his cloak to a beggar. The monastery ran a school here. Some of the oldest parts are thirteenth century.

There were many **gates** at Ely, including three significant entrances from the High Street and a series of smaller pedestrian gates around the precinct. **Steeplegate**, built in the early sixteenth century, was the entrance to the parish burial ground. A predecessor may possibly have been the 'tower of St Peter' which was struck by lightning in 1111 and miraculously saved by the intervention of Etheldreda. The **Porta**, which gave access to what might be termed the outer court of the monastery with its predominantly agricultural and estates activities, was the grandest and was begun in 1397 *(Fig. 76)*. Its walls were constructed in limestone and greensand rubble, which was originally plastered to present a neat appearance. Its upper rooms appear to have been used for the administration of justice (see p. **92**).

A great **barn** of *c.*1400 (labelled as 'stores and granary' on the plan) is now the dining hall of the King's School. It is 51 metres long and has a wonderful medieval roof *(Fig. 74)*. Where the slit windows survive they imply an area for the storage of grain. But some of the surviving medieval windows are of a more domestic type, suggesting that the building was subdivided for

a range of uses from the start.

The King's School, which takes its name from the new foundation of Henry VIII in 1541, represents a tradition of educating children in Ely that stretches back into the pre-Conquest period. Today it occupies many of the monastic buildings and since the last war has educated the cathedral choristers.

The **bishop's palace** was rebuilt by Bishop Alcock *c.*1490 and extended with a long gallery to the north by Bishop Goodrich in 1549–50. It was extensively rebuilt in the late seventeenth century.

Cherry Hill is likely to be the motte of the castle built by the Normans after 1072 and reinforced by Bishop Nigel in the 1130s. It later fell out of military use and became the site of the monastic windmill.

75. The bishop's palace seen from the west tower. In the foreground is the gatehouse of Bishop Alcock (1486–1500), balanced by a symmetrical but somewhat later tower to the west. The long gallery of Bishop Goodrich (1534–54) built c.1549–50 stretches westward. It is an early example of a feature that was to become a standard element of Elizabethan and Jacobean great houses. The E-shaped south range that links the towers was built by Bishop Laney (1667–75).

7. Late Medieval Ely

The fifteenth century is a busy period at Ely in which the cathedral is over-hauled. The western crossing is reinforced in the first decade and in the 1470s further work is prompted by structural collapse. The main transepts are given spectacular hammer-beam roofs in about 1430 and in the following decade new tombs are built in the presbytery. In the late 1480s the windows of the tribunes in the nave are rebuilt. After the election of Bishop Alcock in 1486 a spectacular chantry chapel is put up in the presbytery and a new palace is built at the west end. Alcock's successor, Nicholas West, follows his example with the building of an equally remarkable chapel, finished in 1534.

The fifteenth-century works

The Porta

The opening of the fifteenth century found Ely's builders at work on a major enterprise, the construction of a new gatehouse at the southern end of the precinct. The Porta *(Fig. 76)*, begun in 1397 under the direction of the resident mason John of Meppershall, is by far the largest of the surviving gates. It contained (in addition to the porter's lodge and prison on the ground floor) upper chambers in which the prior and auditor held their courts. The gate arch is guarded by little men-at-arms with swords and bucklers. Security and justice seem to be the principal functions of the building. Prior Buckton, who began it in the last years of his life, would have had painful memories of the Peasants' Revolt. In 1381 the small merchants of Ely had risen against their monastic overlords and had preached rebellion from the cathedral pulpit. They had killed a local lawyer and a justice, and had destroyed some of the abbey's

documents, including court rolls. Their cause was, ostensibly, the king and the common people. The inner elevation of the Porta has shields with the arms of the see as well as those attributed to Edward the Confessor and used at this period by Richard II. They made the point, perhaps, that the justice exercised by the prior was also that of the king.

Perpendicular tracery

This is the earliest building at Ely in which the Perpendicular style makes an appearance. Until this time Ely's builders had found no use for the angular and grid-like tracery, which after 1360 was the fashionable dress of nearly all advanced work *(e.g. Fig. 77)*. For example, the windows introduced into the aisles of Northwold's pres-bytery by Bishop Barnet and others after 1357 were elaborate improvisations on the flowing patterns of the earlier bays to the west. At the Porta, Meppershall was under no such con-straints and we can recognise in the tracery of his windows, and in the pitch of his great arches, the new, hard style of English late gothic.

Reinforcing the western crossing

It was not long before Meppershall became involved in the architecture of the cathedral itself, where there were evidently anxieties about the stability of the west tower. Between 1405 and 1407, he was contracted to strengthen the north side of the west tower with a new arch. It was part of a considerable undertaking in which all four arches of the western crossing *(Fig. 23)* were massively thickened with new masonry. This avoided a repeat of the dreadful 1322 collapse at the eastern crossing or a calamity like that of Bury St Edmunds, where the twelfth-century west tower fell down in two main sections between 1430 and 1432. It did not, however, pre-empt the collapse of the

76. The Porta (begun 1397).

north-west transept. In 1405–7 this transept was probably still standing as the new north arch was designed to open into it, but its days were numbered.

The eastern transept roofs

Within the next two decades the Ely monks were to experience problems with the roofs of the eastern transepts. These had been rebuilt, at the time that the octagon was constructed, on an unusual pattern making use of a broken pitch rather like a mansard roof. This had evidently not lasted well. A tree-ring analysis of the south transept roof has yielded a felling date of *c.*1430. This useful datum probably fixes the identical north transept roof *(Col. pl. 12)*. These hammer-beam roofs were heavily repaired in the nineteenth century when many of the lost angels were replaced. The painted decoration is a Victorian restoration of the medieval scheme (1849 in the south transept and 1857 in the north).

TWO FIFTEENTH-CENTURY TOMBS

There is not much evidence of work by the bishops at this time and there are very few episcopal tombs. Bishop Barnet (1366–73) had left a table tomb of startling simplicity, its sides decorated with repeated quatrefoils. His successor, Thomas Arundel (whose important addition to the palace does not survive), was translated to York in 1388 and then Canterbury. Bishop Fordham (1388–1425) chose, like Simon Montacute, to be buried in the Lady chapel. His tomb, 'in the middle of the chapel towards the east', may have been removed when the chapel became a parish church in the sixteenth century.

Bishop Morgan (1426–34) was buried in the London Charterhouse. One of his executors was John, Baron Tiptoft, a Cambridgeshire landowner with powerful interests at court. He and the Ely chapter now attempted to secure the bishopric for Thomas Bourchier, bishop of Worcester. As was so often the case this local initiative was frustrated by the king who thought Louis de Luxembourg, archbishop of Rouen, a more deserving recipient of this valuable see.

Luxembourg died at the bishop's palace at Hatfield in 1443. His entrails were buried in St Etheldreda's, Hatfield; his heart went to Rouen and his body was brought to Ely, where it was given a handsome tomb in the south-east bay of the presbytery. Its much-restored details are confirmed in an eighteenth-century engraving but the effigy, which does not fit, may well come from another bishop's tomb.

Tiptoft's ambitions of the previous decade were now fulfilled as Bourchier succeeded to the see of Ely in 1443. But he may not have lived to congratulate the new bishop, because it was in this year that Tiptoft died and was buried in a grand tomb evidently designed by the mason of the Luxembourg monument *(Fig. 77)*. The

77. (left) Tomb of John, Baron Tiptoft (died 1443) and his two wives. The tomb of Bishop Redman (1501–5) is visible in the distance. (above) Bishop Louis de Luxembourg's tomb was evidently designed by the mason of Tiptoft's monument. (Engraving from J. Bentham, The History and Antiquities of the Cathedral and Conventual Church of Ely, *1812)*

mutilated and much-restored effigy of Tiptoft displays the SS collar of the house of Lancaster, to which he had been a firm adherent since his exile in France with Bolingbroke in the reign of Richard II. He is flanked by his two wives, Philippa and Joyce, whose divergent ages are indicated in their more and less fashionable costume.

Further problems with the west tower

Bourchier was translated to Canterbury in 1454 and the monastic chronicler records that after his departure he gave 'a hundred marks for the repair of our belltower'. His successor, William Gray (1454–78) also gave money towards the repair of the tower and these donations by the bishops are probably connected with some documented repair work on the west tower in 1474/5. By this time, the north-west transept had probably given way. A mass of twelfth-century masonry, sufficient for the support of one of the crossing piers, still stands today on the east side, but nothing remains to the north and west. Here it was necessary to build a great raking buttress *(Fig. 23)*. The masonry courses of the buttress do not line up with those of Meppershall's arch so it must be later, and the plinth is decorated with tracery and shields in a distinctly late fifteenth-century manner. The heraldry has been largely obliterated but the arms of the see of Ely are clear and probably refer to the help given by the bishops in this emergency of the 1470s. Bishop Gray was buried in the presbytery in 1478 and the design of his tomb, of which fragments survive, is recorded in an eighteenth-century engraving.

It is interesting that none of his successors thought fit to make good the loss of the north-west transept but occupied themselves in other more agreeable personal projects. Bishop John Morton (1479–86) built himself a new palace at Hatfield whose surviving great hall is an excellent example of contemporary brickwork. He

also rebuilt the bishop's castle at Wisbech and dug a mighty navigable drainage channel, Morton's Leam, from Guyhirn to Peterborough. It was 19 kilometres long. Before his translation to Canterbury he played an important part in the conclusion of the Wars of the Roses by negotiating the marriage contract between Henry Tudor and Elizabeth, daughter of the Yorkist king Edward IV, in 1485.

BISHOP ALCOCK'S CHANTRY

John Alcock, who succeeded Morton at Ely in 1486, was a Yorkshireman and a fervent and well-rewarded supporter of Edward IV. It was under 'this sun of York' that he had become successively bishop of Rochester, then of Worcester; lord president of Wales and, for a while, lord chancellor. He was famously devout, using his ample means to endow a series of religious and educational projects. At Ely he built a new bishop's palace and a remarkable chantry chapel.

The chantry *(Figs. 78 and 79)* has long been admired for its rich architectural effect but when examined closely it reveals a multitude of puzzling irregularities which very nearly defy analysis. An inscribed slab, recovered in the eighteenth century from a grave some distance away, is thought to be its foundation stone and is dated 1488. Chantries were established to endow priests who would say masses, often in perpetuity, for the souls of the donor. This system appeared very early at Ely, in the thirteenth-century chantry foundation of Bishop Northwold, and came gradually to supplant the monastic system of memorial masses. By Alcock's time it was seen as quite the most effective means by which the wealthy could reduce the period of agony and torment which their souls must spend in purgatory. To an extent all the charitable institutions created by Alcock arose from this consideration, because good

78. Bishop Alcock's chantry (1480s).

but the walls of the chantry, by contrast, look like an attempt to get a quart into a pint pot. The distinctive design element is the use of square tabernacles, set diagonally and supporting spires of openwork tracery. Such a thing has no precedent in England. The openwork spire is a German device that can also be found in some late French and Spanish work. Alcock's chapel displays other cosmopolitan features which, taken together, make the incompetence of the planning the more surprising.

At the corners, the great tabernacles crash into one another *(Fig. 79)*. Ornamental features have to be omitted in order to allow major elements to fit together, and the faces of the tabernacles hidden from view by their neighbours are left half carved. One or two little sculpted figures have escaped the attention of the iconoclasts merely because they are trapped, and partially hidden, by colliding tabernacle work. In the upper levels there is a substantial decorative openwork parapet (similar to that above Bishop Redman's tomb) which can hardly be seen at all because of the choking thicket of spires and pinnacles.

What has happened here? This muddle is wholly uncharacteristic of late gothic design, in which the orderly relationship of parts nearly always controls the most complex of schemes. There are several clues. On the internal north wall, which houses the tomb, a little door leads nowhere and suggests that the chapel might have been designed for another location altogether. On the west elevation it has been necessary to cut away a large section of the aisle wall to display the full width of the chantry. On the south side there is a large archway *(Fig. 78)* which is set off-centre in an architectural composition in which a whole section of panelling is missing from the eastern end. It is also very noticeable that the spires and pinnacles sit most unhappily under the vault. If these complex walls had been set out on a larger plan it might have been possible to accommodate all

works were thought to have a marginal but significant effect on God's mercy.

Alcock used the north-east bay of Northwold's presbytery for his chapel. He demolished the thirteenth-century vaulting and inserted a beautiful fan vault with an elaborate hanging central boss decorated, like those of central Europe, with skeletal ribs. It shows every sign of being carefully integrated with its setting

79. Canopies in Alcock's chantry.

these elements in a more coherent scheme.

This expansion, impossible in the relatively confined presbytery bays at Ely, might have worked in the more generous proportions of the presbytery at Worcester cathedral where Alcock had been bishop before his translation to Ely. Could the chantry have been prepared initially for Worcester? A detail which suggests that the chantry walls may pre-date Alcock's translation is excessive use of the *Rose-en-Soleil* badge of Edward IV, who died in 1483. This device, a rose superimposed on a sunburst, peppers the cornices and terminates the pendant drops of the canopies. It has to be admitted, however, that it is also used in the vault which, as we have seen, must have been built for Ely. The mason employed by Bishop Alcock for this work and for the new palace may have been Adam

Lord whom he paid in June 1490 a yearly allowance of £2 and a daily rate of 8d so long as he remained at Ely.

The Lady chapel vault and the nave tribune windows

The Tudor rose, a double flower combining the white and red flowers of York and Lancaster, is the badge devised by Henry VII to celebrate the conjunction of two rival dynasties in his marriage to Elizabeth of York in 1485. Francis Woodman has drawn attention to the appearance of these double roses in the side bosses of the great lierne vault of the Lady chapel. He has suggested that the vault, which fits badly on its supports, may not have been built until the 1480s. One difficulty with this idea is that many of the other bosses look fourteenth century. It is not impossible, of course, that a fifteenth-century vault could make use of some bosses that had been prepared for the purpose many years earlier. On the other hand, roses of various kinds are used in earlier work (see the tomb of Bishop de Luda and the junctions of the eastern arches in Northwold's presbytery, the west door and some of the fourteenth-century misericords). It is an intriguing problem, but if such a late date for the vault is correct this was a busy decade at the cathedral. A year after Alcock's enthronement, in 1487–8, battlements were added to the south side of the nave. This could have marked the completion of the extensive campaign in which the outer tribune walls on both sides of the nave were given new three-light windows.

Alcock's palace and alterations in the Galilee

The beautiful iron gates on the west entrance to Alcock's chantry are original, and identical in detail to a pair of displaced gates in the south porch. It is recorded that Alcock contributed two gates or doors to the cathedral. Those now in the south porch *(Fig. 89)* are the right size to have formed part of a substantial in-filling of the Galilee porch entrance which is recorded in an early eighteenth-century engraving *(Fig. 80)*. This small but significant change in the west front might have been connected with a much larger plan in which the building of Alcock's new palace, south of the west front, created a most impressive architectural ensemble.

Rising to answer the mass of the Galilee porch is a handsome Tudor gatehouse whose arch (long since removed) was surmounted by niches in a field of diapered brickwork. The original gate passage is spanned by a fine lierne vault. In the ring of bosses surrounding the centrepiece of the bishop's arms, the badge of Edward IV is repeated, but now incorporating the double flower of the Tudors. Alcock's reputation for piety was no doubt enhanced by the numerous improving texts which once decorated the glazing of both the Ely palace and the smaller residence at nearby Downham, which he also rebuilt. The Ely palace included a new hall and a 'gallery'. This gallery has been interpreted by many authorities as the building that once linked the palace to the south-west transept of the cathedral. A smaller surviving gallery can be seen at Corpus Christi College, Cambridge, where it connects the former master's lodge to St Bene't's church, which served as the college chapel. It was in Cambridge that Alcock began, in 1495, his greatest charitable foundation, Jesus College.

Alcock's death in 1500 made way for Richard Redman, then bishop of Exeter, a member of the Privy Council. The tomb and chantry in which he was buried in 1505 have many points of intimate correspondence with the more conventional parts of Alcock's chapel. James Stanley, who was installed as bishop in 1506, did little of consequence at Ely but improved the palace at Somersham where he lived in some comfort with the woman who bore him three children. This inappropriate lifestyle and his generally notorious immorality provided ammunition for Protestant tract writers. He may have been exceptional but a decline in standards amongst the clergy and the monastic orders was widespread at this time. The sorry moral and physical condition of St Radegund's nunnery in Cambridge had enabled Alcock to suppress it without difficulty in order to found Jesus College. Somewhat later, Thomas Wolsey was able to close a whole group of religious houses in order to fund the creation of Cardinal College at Oxford. These suppressions could be regarded as the beginning of a long-overdue internal reform of the medieval Church in which colleges, already more active intellectually, might gradually have come to supplant monasteries as the engines of theology and devotion. Something more radical and more violent was, however, looming into view.

BISHOP WEST AND HIS CHANTRY

The ceremony at which Wolsey received his cardinal's hat was presided over by Stanley's successor at Ely, Nicholas West, who was a brilliant diplomat and dean of Windsor. His great moment came when he managed to seal a defensive alliance with France and to persuade Francis I to pay a debt of one million crowns [£250,000], owed by his predecessor to Henry VIII. Wolsey saw that West was rewarded for this triumph with the bishopric of Ely in 1515. In the spring of the following year, the new bishop conducted a visitation to the monastery. In a letter to Wolsey he wrote that he 'found such disorder at Ely that but for this visit it could not have been continued a monastery four years'. Against this image of an institution in terminal decline we have evidence of an extensive rebuilding campaign in the cloisters, whose east walk was finished in 1509/10 at a cost of over £124.

Bishop West's own experience of building was considerable. He had overseen the completion of St George's chapel between 1509 and 1511. Its architectural details are reflected in the chantry chapel that he built at his native Putney, where his father is said to have been a baker. West lived in great state, and it was said that he employed over a hundred servants. He is also reputed to have fed over two hundred poor people with cooked food each day. At Ely, early in the 1520s, he began a second chantry chapel whose sophisticated design and sumptuous detailing is a similar combination of luxury and piety *(Fig. 81)*. There is some disagreement about whether the architect was John Lee, who worked with John Wastell on the completion of King's College chapel, or Richard Lee. The latter is mentioned in a letter written from Ely to Thomas Cromwell (soon to mastermind the Dissolution of the Monasteries), in which he is recommended for a secret mission: 'an honest man, Richard Lee, a free mason, whom ye right well know'. He appears again as the overseer of the will of the sculptor Edmund More, who died in 1536. More undertook the figure sculpture of West's chapel between 1523 and 1533, and purchased a house in Ely for the duration. Like West, More was a man at the centre of things. From his other house, at Kingston, he worked at Hampton Court Palace after the fall of Wolsey, carving heraldic achievements and the wooden stalls of the royal chapel.

West's chantry at Ely, whose completion in 1534 is attested by an inscription over the entrance, is a most exciting document of the reception of Renaissance decorative ideas into a native late gothic that was still vital and developing. The natural intermingling of the two traditions is most noticeable in the vault where the webs of a gothic stellar rib pattern, related to the chapel vault at Hampton Court, are filled with Renaissance motifs of putti and sprays of foliage. In the little friezes on the north wall, moreover, are trails of decorative foliage in

which there is a series of figures locked in combat. These have been shown to come from Renaissance ornaments in a Book of Hours printed in Paris by Pingonchet in 1497 and repeated in another Book of Hours of 1511 by Antoine Verard. The glorious niche work, however, is entirely gothic and supremely confident in its setting out. It shows up the chaos in Alcock's chapel on the other side of the presbytery.

West, keen perhaps to avoid the cramping problems of this earlier chantry, actually pushed out beyond the envelope of the thirteenth-century work to provide a setting for the east window *(Fig. 52)*. This is a characteristically

80. The western façade of the Galilee porch before its alteration by Bernasconi in 1802. (From B. Willis, A Survey of the Cathedrals of Lincoln, Ely, Oxford and Peterborough, 1730)

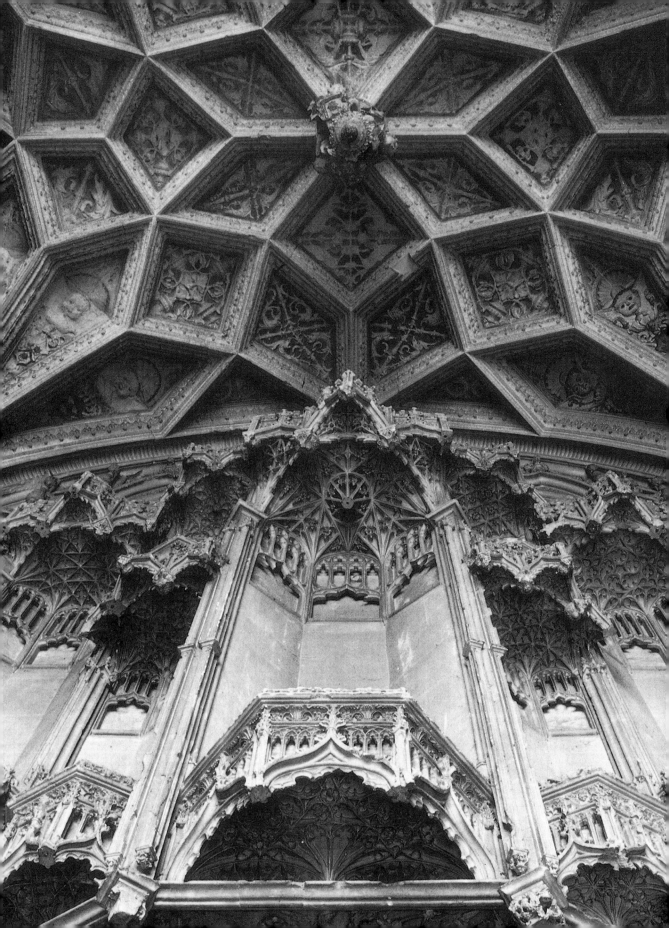

elegant piece of Perpendicular design but Lee had clearly offered his patron a choice of patterns. Four rejects, each very much the equal of what was built, are offered in miniature on the panels flanking the altar. This delight in variation can also be seen in the miniature lierne vaults of the numerous sculpture tabernacles, where every rib pattern appears to be different. The loss of More's sculpture at the Reformation is almost too painful to contemplate. We can only speculate as to whether it was wholly northern and gothic in character or whether it was in part Renaissance. There is one place where the iconoclasts were careless, and that is in the external panel that fills the arch above the adjacent Luxembourg tomb. Here large angels kneel on either side of a little, barefoot seraph.

Originally there were two types of inscription in the chapel. The one that survives is the Latin motto from St Paul, repeated many times: *Gracia Dei Sum Id Quod Sum* (by the grace of God I am what I am). It was a comment on West's humble origins and immense wealth. The other,

now lost, was in English. It conveyed a more urgent message:

> Of your charitie pray for the soule of Richard West, sometime Bishop of this See, and for all Christian soules; in the which prayer he hath granted to every person so doing 40 days of pardon for every time they shall so pray.

This reciprocal system of intercession and redemption was already falling into disrepute, as was the whole doctrine of purgatory. Indulgences of the type offered by West were often granted for contributions to building work. Those given by the pope in return for compulsory contributions to the building of St Peter's basilica led to Martin Luther's famous ninety-five objections. This was in 1517. Within little more than thirty years all the English chantries were abolished, the monasteries were closed and 90 per cent of the art of the medieval Church was carted away or smashed *in situ*. By the time of West's death in 1533 the storm was about to break.

81. (left) Bishop West's chantry. Amongst the tabernacles and in the webs of the vault the gothic architecture readily accommodates the new Renaissance ornament. The disciplined gothic framework hides an extraordinary variety in the details.

8. REFORMATION

The monastery is dissolved in 1539 when the shrines and other valuable devotional objects are destroyed. The re-establishment of the cathedral and the replacement of the monastic community with a college takes place in 1541. Further iconoclasm follows in 1547 with the accession of Edward VI. Catholicism is reintroduced by Mary Tudor in 1553 and Bishop Thirlby goes to Rome to submit the country to papal authority. Protestants are burnt in Ely. The accession of Elizabeth in 1558 introduces a period of stability in which the Protestant faith is re-established and iconoclasm is controlled and tempered. The Lady chapel becomes the parish church of Holy Trinity.

In 1534 Henry VIII nominated Thomas Goodrich to the see of Ely. Goodrich had already been useful to the king as one of the syndics of the University of Cambridge who had asserted the illegitimacy of his marriage to Katherine of Aragon. It was because the pope would not accept the ensuing divorce that Henry devised the Act of Supremacy 1534, which did away with papal authority in England. In 1535 Goodrich was encouraging the preaching of the doctrine of supremacy in parish churches and college chapels throughout his diocese.

With the pope out of the way, the king could now do what he liked with the monasteries and their great estates.

THE DISSOLUTION AT ELY AND THE FIRST ICONOCLASM

The lesser monasteries were dissolved in 1536, and between 1537 and 1540 most of the larger ones gave themselves up without resistance. On

18 November 1539 Robert Wells (later called Steward), who had been prior since 1522, surrendered Ely to the king's commissioners. He was a willing agent of the change and persuaded other local abbots to fall in with the king's demands. These included giving up the shrines and other valuable treasures of the Church. Shrines and miracle-working images were regarded by Archbishop Cranmer and others as the focus of unhealthy superstition and by the king as a ready source of funds. The great weight of gold and jewels confiscated from Ely at this time is recorded in the account of Sir John Williams, the king's master and treasurer of the jewels. Dr John Caius (founder of the Cambridge college) recalled, with some satisfaction, the destruction of Etheldreda's shrine:

Although the blindness of that age bred admiration therein, yet when the tomb was pluckt down in the reign of King Henry the Eighth it was found to be made of common stone, and not of white marble, as Bede reporteth. Thus was her tomb degraded and debased one degree, which makes the truth of all the rest to be suspected. And if all Popish miracles were brought to the test, they would be found to shrink from marble to common stone, nay from stone to untempered dirt and mortar.

This destruction was not necessarily part of a reformation of the cathedral as a whole. The shrines and miracle-working images were targeted first. Goodrich and others had however shown their true colours in writing the so-called 'Bishops' Book', *The Godly and Pious Institution of Christian Man*, of 1537. This took its authority from the Second Commandment in issuing a general prohibition against the making of images. The king, who was very attached to his Catholic faith, attempted to temper this measure in his own revision, the 'King's Book', but this tinkering could not halt the chain reaction which he had begun.

The new cathedral foundation

Now that the saints' bodies had been removed, Ely was founded afresh, in 1541, as the Cathedral Church of the Holy and Undivided Trinity. New statutes established, in place of the monastery, a college. It was partly composed of members of the old community. Instead of a prior and obedientiaries there was to be a dean and a group of eight canons or prebendaries. There were also eight minor canons, most of whom were former monks, four divinity students, eight singing men and eight choristers. There were twenty-four grammar school boys, 'six aged men decayed in the King's Warres or Service' (bedesmen charged with praying for the king and doing odd jobs), and one or two masters and officials.

The residences and offices of the obedientaries were now carved up between the prebendaries. Three names stand out. Richard Cox was given the first canonry (the cellarer's lodging).

Matthew Parker took the second (Alan of Walsingham's Painted Chamber) and William Maye was ensconced in the third (the Black Hostelry). Parker, who had belonged to a Lutheran circle in his student days, was a moderate destined for the archbishopric of Canterbury in the reign of Elizabeth. Cox and Maye, on the other hand, were convinced

82. *The gilt-bronze seal matrixes of Henry VIII's new cathedral foundation of 1541 display the Holy Trinity (the new dedication) and the king enthroned. The arms of the see lie, symbolically, at the king's feet.*

Protestants whose activities were to be central to the iconoclastic reign of Edward VI. There is no doubt that Bishop Goodrich was also a keen reformer. In prosecuting the injunctions against shrines and miracle-working images in his diocese, he went beyond the king's instructions by requesting certificates signed by three parishioners to prove that the job had been done.

Iconoclasm under Edward VI

It is generally thought that Richard Cox, as tutor and almoner to Edward VI, turned the young king's mind to the completion of the Reformation initiated by his father. Henry VIII had passed the Act suppressing chantries in 1545 but relatively little damage had been done before his son succeeded in 1547. In that year the chantry endowments were diverted to other educational and charitable purposes. New and more comprehensive injunctions were sent out to cathedrals. These instructed deans to destroy all shrines, tables, candlesticks, pictures, paintings and other monuments of idolatry. It was very probably in 1547 that Dean Steward deprived Ely of the hundreds of statues and other images that decorated the building inside and out. What could not be removed was defaced, and the bruised and broken remains were given a coat of whitewash to tidy up the mess. The thoroughness with which this job was carried out is striking – especially in the Lady chapel, whose cultic function was anathema to the reformers and where the soft stone of the wall arcades yielded readily to hammers and axes *(Fig. 83)*.

It is unlikely that Maye and Cox, both of whom were busy reinforcing the Reformation in other dioceses and in the universities, could have devoted a great deal of time to the reform of Ely. But as members of chapter they could hardly have assented to anything other than an exemplary cleansing there. Miraculously, the

Etheldreda reliefs in the octagon survived completely unscathed. Lindley plausibly attributes this phenomenon to the large number of crowned, royal figures represented in the scenes. Goodrich and Steward were probably reluctant to order their destruction when Henry had so recently established the king's pre-eminence as head of the Church.

In 1549 the Latin mass was abolished and Cranmer's Prayer Book was introduced. It was

83. Lady chapel wall arcade. The cult of the Virgin was a target for reformers. All the free-standing figures in the Lady chapel would have been destroyed in the reign of Edward VI, when the cycle of reliefs illustrating the life of the Virgin would also have been defaced. Those represented here show Three Shepherds of Joachim, and Joachim meeting Anne at the Temple Gate.

GOODRICH'S BRASS

Goodrich built himself a handsome long gallery at the palace (Fig. 75) but, for obvious reasons, there were no significant additions at the cathedral in his time. He is commemorated by a brass (Fig. 84) which now lies in the south choir aisle. It is an ambiguous monument that could easily be mistaken for a pre-Reformation effigy. His pontifical vestments are, if anything, more elaborate than those shown on earlier medieval bishops' brasses. In one hand he holds his crosier and in the other a richly bound book. The book is probably the New Testament in English. Until Mary's reign, this New Testament had given congregations the direct access to scripture which had been denied in medieval Catholicism. Goodrich had contributed the revised translation of John's gospel. Dangling from his finger is the Great Seal, entrusted to him as chancellor. The lost Latin inscription contained none of the late medieval requests for intercessions. It merely recorded his life and ended with the defiant reformer's text from Paul's letter to the Romans: 'If God is with us, who can be against us.'

84. Bishop Goodrich's brass (c.1554).

revised in 1552 in a version that removed from the new communion service the identification of the bread and wine with the body and blood of Christ. Goodrich, who was made lord chancellor in January of that year, sat in the Parliament that made this new liturgy into law. The death of Edward in 1553 brought in the nine-day reign of Lady Jane Grey, during which Goodrich remained. After its violent end and the accession of Mary Tudor, he was imprisoned and removed from office. None the less, because he opposed a rebellion by the duke of Northumberland and did homage to the new queen, he was allowed to keep his bishopric. In the following year, however, he died.

MARY TUDOR AND BISHOP THIRLBY: THE BURNING OF PROTESTANT MARTYRS

The new bishop appointed by Mary was Thomas Thirlby, who had begun as a favourite of Cranmer but had gradually become 'unsound' on one or two key Reformation issues. Mary sent Thirlby as an ambassador to Rome in 1554/5 to reassert England's obedience to papal authority. As the whole machinery of religion was now thrown into reverse, efforts must have been made at Ely to restore some key images and other furnishings of the Catholic rite. In the second year of Thirlby's episcopate three local Protestant heretics were tried in Ely before a group that included his chancellor Thomas Fuller and the dean, Robert Steward. William Wolsey and the painter Robert Pigot, both from Wisbech, were brought to Ely and imprisoned. Pigot was asked to save his life by signing a statement that he believed the bread and wine changed into the body and blood of Christ at the consecration but, according to Foxe's *Book of Martyrs*:

> 'No sir', said the painter, 'that is your faith not mine' … Pigot and Wolsey being brought to the place of execution and bound with a chain, cometh one to the fire with a great sheet knit full of books to burn, like as they had been New Testaments. 'Oh', said Wolsey, 'give me one of them' and Pigot desired another; both of them clapping them close to their breasts, saying the 106th psalm, desiring all the people to say Amen; and so received the fire most thankfully.

In the same year Thirlby took part in the trial of his former protector, Cranmer. He protested with tears in his eyes that this was 'the most sorrowful action of his whole life' and that 'no earthly consideration but the queen's command could have induced him to come to what they were then about'. Clearly Thirlby could not have remained long in post after the accession of Elizabeth in 1558. He opposed the reintroduction of Protestant reforms and, having refused to take the Oath of Supremacy, was ejected from his see in 1559. His continued sermons against the Reformation put him in the Tower.

Dean Steward had been succeeded by Andrew Perne in 1557. Five times chancellor of the University of Cambridge and master of Peterhouse, Perne lived through these troubled times and continued to hold prestigious offices by changing his public utterances to conform with whatever regime happened to be in power. In 1556 he preached the sermon when the dead bodies of the two German scholars Fagius and

Bucer, who had been condemned as heretics, were burnt with a pile of Protestant books, but four years later he presided over the Cambridge Senate which restored their honours. This was merely the most breath-taking of a series of U-turns which inspired the Elizabethan invention of a new Latin verb: *pernare*, to turn, rat or change often.

During his tenure at Ely, Perne must have negotiated the removal of the parish of Holy Trinity from their 'very uncomely and noisome and dangerous … lean-to' on the north side of the nave to the now redundant Lady chapel. The parishioners had been so unhappy with their accommodation that they were prepared to go to law in 1566 to secure an improvement. But for its new use as a parish church, the Lady chapel would, like its predecessor at Peterborough, have fallen into ruin and been demolished.

BISHOP COX AND ELIZABETHAN ELY

Dr Richard Cox, who had spent Mary's reign in exile – first in Frankfurt and then in Zurich and Worms – was appointed Thirlby's successor at Ely. He did little to ingratiate himself, however, and refused to minister in the queen's chapel because of the crucifix and candles there. To reformers, candles implied superstitious ritual. It is uncertain whether he approved of the royal proclamation of September 1560 which complained of the 'defacing of monuments of antiquity, being set up in churches or in other public places for memory and not for superstition'. It required that 'no such barbarous disorder be here after used' and urged people 'to repair as much of the said monuments as conveniently may be'.

This is an important witness to the developing historical sensibility of Elizabeth's reign in response to the extensive Protestant destruction of tombs, targeted because their inscriptions invited supplications for the benefit of souls. The fact that Goodrich's brass survives and that the other bishops' brasses at Ely have been torn from their slabs may imply that these other 'graven images' had all gone before Goodrich's brass was commissioned after 1551. In 1568 the Privy Council issued a letter requiring the preservation of historical documents. The direction of this work was given to Cox's former Ely colleague Matthew Parker (now archbishop of Canterbury) who sent out his agents to gather from the book trade and elsewhere the scattered manuscripts of the dissolved monasteries. Many found their way into college libraries including Parker's own magnificent collection now at Corpus Christi, Cambridge.

The new tombs that began to appear in the cathedral at this time are in some ways the products of this more conservative regard for the past. Sir Robert Steward (who died in 1570), whose relationship to the eponymous former Dean had given him some very profitable local leases, has a fine monument *(Col. pl. 13)*. His armoured figure reclines on one elbow in a tabard of bewildering heraldic complexity very typical of the period.

The queen's innate conservatism led her to attempt the reintroduction of the pre-Reformation ban on clergy marriages on the ground that the presence of women would be an unhealthy distraction. Cox, who like many Protestant divines was married, resisted vociferously and in doing so gave us a memorable image of post-Reformation Ely:

> in these vast cathedral churches with their rooms plenty and several, on what ground should this be ordained? I have but one prebendary continually resident in Ely Church. Turn him out and daws and owls may dwell there for my continual housekeeping.

Such outbursts did him no good. He was passed over for the archbishopric when Parker died in 1575 and in the same year, to his intense annoyance, Sir Christopher Hatton was able to use the queen's influence to acquire the Ely estate in Holborn. In 1579/80 a disgruntled Cox retired to live the remainder of his life on a pension of £200 at the palace of Doddington. The rare contemporary painting that depicts his splendid funeral in 1581 *(Col. pl. 13)* is a most important record of post-Reformation funerary customs. The sombre heraldic draperies and the canopied bier shown are often depicted in medieval manuscripts. But whereas the medieval biers are usually covered in a forest of candles and surrounded by tapers, not one light is visible at the funeral of Bishop Cox.

9. ELY IN THE SEVENTEENTH CENTURY

This troubled period begins with a return to more ritualistic liturgical practice and the appointment of bishops like Lancelot Andrewes and Matthew Wren. After the outbreak of war in 1642, Ely is saved from another wave of iconoclasm by Oliver Cromwell, who interrupts the cathedral's services in 1644. There are demolitions in the precinct after the parliamentary survey of 1650 but the cathedral itself survives and is extensively repaired after the Restoration of the monarchy in 1660. The collapse of the main north transept in 1699 brings the century to a dramatic close.

SEVENTEENTH-CENTURY BISHOPS

After the resignation of Bishop Cox the queen decided not to fill the vacancy, and for eighteen years she received the revenues of the see. This ended with the election in 1599 of Bishop Martin Heton, the former dean of Winchester. Elizabeth was not keen to give up the income she had received and so made Heton's post conditional on the surrender to her of some of the most valuable remaining estates. Other candidates had rejected the bishopric on this account but it is thought that Heton had little say in the matter. After his death in 1609 his two daughters put up a handsome monument with an effigy in alabaster of this fine preacher and distinguished theologian. The bishop's corpulent features represent the first attempt at a true portrait in the cathedral *(Fig. 85)*. Heton wears the vestments prescribed by the ornaments rubric in the Elizabethan Prayer Book of 1559. This put an end to medieval mass vestments such as those worn by Goodrich on his brass nearby. In cathe-

drals those celebrating communion were now to wear a surplice and a cope, a provision seen by more extreme Protestants as conservative and popish. The bishop's cope is indeed strongly medieval in character (compare *Col. pl. 10*). Edged with a rich orphrey, decorated with figures of the apostles under gothic canopies, it is one of the many signs in early seventeenth-century England that the task of the reformers had yet to be fully accomplished.

Lancelot Andrewes, who was elected to Ely after Heton's death, was one of the most formidable scholars of his time and a spiritual leader of great integrity. The furnishings of his private chapel were rich and he was noted for his religious liberalism. His successor, John Buckeridge, elected in 1628, held similar views. Under Charles I all new bishops were selected for their opposition to Puritan tendencies and in 1638 Matthew Wren was translated to Ely from Norwich.

Wren was one of several bishops who denied Calvin's doctrine of predestination and held

OLIVER CROMWELL

Oliver Cromwell moved to Ely from St Ives and took over the house which had been built in the former sacrist's grange. It was a turning point for Cromwell, who awoke from a fit of depression to discover the deep religious convictions that were to sustain his remarkable career. 'But whether', as Christopher Hill has written, 'there was any connection between the riches of uncle Thomas Steward and the riches of God's mercy we shall probably never know.' In 1640 Cromwell was elected to Parliament for Cambridge and two years later Parliament and the king were at war. By 1643 Cromwell had assembled at Huntingdon a regiment of horse noted for its strict discipline and orderly behaviour. These troops were part of a larger and more excitable parliamentary army which in April of that year sacked Peterborough cathedral. The targets of the soldiers were ancient and modern examples of popery. They indulged in an orgy of destruction that indiscriminately included the relatively modern tombs of local Elizabethan gentry whose immediate descendants would have been well known to the Cromwells.

Although this kind of incident has fixed Cromwell in the public mind as a vandal, the truth is more complicated. In late August Parliament passed an ordinance requiring the destruction of 'all Monuments of Superstition and Idolatry'. It did, however, contain an important proviso. This exempted images and coats of arms which had been set up 'only for a monument of any king, prince or Nobleman, or other dead person which hath not commonly been taken for a Saint'. It was a restatement of the policy of Queen Elizabeth, whose reign was, for Cromwell, a golden age of co-operation between sovereign and Parliament. If properly applied, it would constrain the indiscriminate destruction which Cromwell had been unable to prevent at Peterborough.

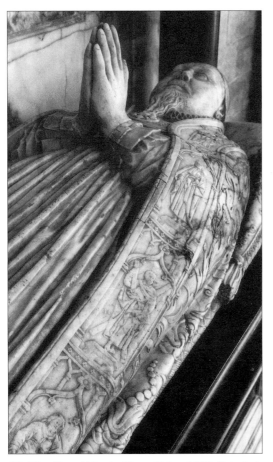

85. The effigy of Martin Heton (bishop 1600–9) is clad in a seventeenth-century gothic cope.

that all Christians, rather than a chosen few, were capable of salvation. The articles of his visitation to the Ely diocese duplicated those which, at Norwich, had already 'raised the puritanism of East Anglia to a dangerous pitch of rebellious fury'. In the minds of the Protestant gentry, cathedrals had come to represent the overweening power of the bishops and their services confirmed, if confirmation were needed, a drift towards popery. In 1636 the man who best represents this class of increasingly indignant landed gentry inherited the lucrative Ely dean and chapter leases that had been farmed by his maternal uncle Sir Thomas Steward.

It is in this context that we have to see Cromwell's famous intervention in Ely cathedral in January 1644 as governor of the Isle of Ely. It began with a short letter to the minor canon, William Hitch, who in the absence of the dean and prebendaries appears to have been running the cathedral from day to day. The letter is not a veiled threat but an expression of genuine concern for the safety of the cathedral, a building which, of course, contained the splendid Elizabethan monuments of Cromwell's maternal relatives, the Stewards.

MR HITCH,

Lest the Soldiers should in any tumultuary or disorderly way attempt the reformation of the Cathedral Church, I require you to forbear altogether your Choir-service, so unedifying and offensive: – – and this as you shall answer it, if any disorder should arise thereupon.

I advise you to catechise, and read and expound the Scripture to the people; not doubting but the Parliament with the advice of the Assembly of Divines, will direct you farther. I desire your Sermons 'too', where they usually have been , – but more frequent. Your loving friend,

OLIVER CROMWELL.

This was friendly advice. When Hitch felt obliged to persist we are told that

Cromwell with a party of soldiers attended by the rabble, came into church in the time of divine service, with his hat on, and directing himself to Mr Hitch, said, 'I am a man under authority and am commanded to dismiss this assembly.' Mr Hitch proceeded with the service, at which Cromwell, laying his hand on his sword in a passion, bade Mr Hitch to 'leave off his fooling and come down' and so drove out the whole congregation.

The building is popularly supposed to have been closed after this incident, but there is no clear evidence that it was. The high liturgical practices curtailed by Cromwell would have been enjoyed by Dean Henry Caesar (1614–36) *(Col. pl. 13)*, whose Roman leanings got him into trouble in the reign of Elizabeth. Incense was used in the cathedral at this time, and in 1618–19 the choir had been refurbished with velvet and with crimson and purple taffeta. The wonderful choral settings which Caesar commissioned from John Amner (cathedral organist, 1610–41) would not be heard again for many years. But Cromwell's action in curbing ritualistic practices seems to have spared Ely the wave of violent reform endured by so many cathedrals and parish churches in the years to come. The earlier Reformation damage had been all too obvious to Lieutenant Hammond, who in 1635 bemoaned the mutilated condition of the sculpture at Ely. But it is perhaps a tribute to Cromwell's protection that when Celia Fiennes recorded her visit in 1698 she could remark 'this Church has the most Popish remains in its walls of any I have seen'.

With the establishment of the Commonwealth after the execution of Charles I commissioners were sent out, in 1650, to inspect the cathedrals on behalf of Parliament. Their detailed survey of the monastic buildings at Ely is of great historical value but it prompted the demolition of the chapter house and the cloisters. Places like Ely were now in great danger. The cathedral had already escaped a plan of 1647/8 to demolish the entire building so that its materials might be sold to benefit 'sick and maimed soldiers, Widows and Orphans'. It was at this time that William Dugdale compiled his great volumes of monastic history, *Monasticon Anglicanum*. The entry on Ely was illustrated with Daniel King's engraving of the cathedral from the north *(Fig. 86)* and the heraldic device in the left-hand corner bears a Latin inscription, translated as 'Lest it perish utterly'.

86. Daniel King's engraving of the cathedral from the north, from William Dugdale's Monasticon Anglicanum *of 1655.*

THE RESTORATION

With the Restoration of the monarchy in 1660 Bishop Wren, who had spent the period of the Commonwealth in prison, was released and returned to his diocese. He gave thanks for his deliverance by building a new chapel at Pembroke College. It was one of the first significant architectural works of his polymath nephew Christopher Wren. There was much for the dean and chapter to do at Ely in the first decades of the Restoration. The choir was refurbished once more with new cushions covered with purple fustian and decorated with gold fringes. Substantial loans were raised from individual chapter members for the repair of the church. It seems that in 1662 the scar created by the demolition of the church of Holy Cross after 1566 (clearly shown in King's engraving) was made good. In this year £1,600 was spent on repairs, in 1664 over £1,900 and in 1669 nearly £3,000. This last was associated with repairs to the troublesome west tower, which was now to receive the bells from the octagon. They had been removed because they were observed to rock the whole structure of the lantern when they were rung. The most conspicuous change at Ely was, however, the rebuilding of much of the palace by Bishop Laney (1667–75) *(Fig. 75)*.

Bishop Peter Gunning, who came to Ely in 1675, hoped that the choir and its stalls might be moved from under the lantern to the east end of the church, but did not live to carry out this scheme. When he died he left £100 for the paving of the choir. He is commemorated in a good monument which lost its architectural backdrop in the nineteenth century. The white marble effigy of the bishop *(Fig. 87)* reclines in a pose of weary wakefulness, similar to Sir Robert Steward's effigy of more than a century earlier. (Both derive ultimately from a much-copied innovation in funerary sculpture by Jacopo Sansovino: the tomb of Cardinal Sforza in S. Maria del Popolo, Rome, of 1505.)

Gunning was a staunch royalist in the Civil War and was thought by many Puritans to be

111

87. Detail of the effigy of Bishop Peter Gunning (died 1684).

88. Dean John Spencer's font of 1693, now in Prickwillow church.

'popish', a charge that is refuted by some of his writings. He died in 1684, a year before the accession of James II. This convinced Catholic attempted to introduce toleration for those of his faith and other dissenters. This was openly opposed by Gunning's successor, Francis Turner, who refused to allow the Declaration of Liberty of Conscience to be read in the Ely diocese. The highly principled Turner lost his bishopric in the Revolution of 1688. Although he was no supporter of the outgoing regime he felt unable to swear allegiance to William III while his oath to James was still in force. The dean at this period was John Spencer (1677–93), a great scholar and the author of ground-breaking studies on comparative religion in the ancient world. He was also interested in beautiful things, it seems, and gave to

the cathedral a remarkable font which is described by Celia Fiennes in 1698:

> The Font is one entire piece of white marble stemme and foote, the Cover was carv'd wood with the image Christs being baptised by John and the holy Dove descending on him, all finely carved white wood without any paint or varnish; they draw up the Cover by a pully

The wonderful cover (recorded in an engraving) has vanished but the font itself went in 1866 to Prickwillow where, in the words of Nikolaus Pevsner, 'It stands in its exquisite white marble beauty ... like a gilt goblet on a poor man's bare boards' *(Fig. 88)*. Celia, who came from a Puritan family, picked up some gossip about the sort of people who were attracted to the cathedral before the Protestant Revolution of 1688.

> This cathedral was much frequented by the priests in King James the Second's tyme and many of their Relicts washed fair to be seen and the woman told me the priest used to shew here where everything was and they hoped quickly to be in possession of it ... but blessed be God that put a tymely stop to the Protestants utter ruin and the hopes of the Papists.

If she had arrived in the year following her visit she would have found an even more exciting subject for her active pen, because on the night of 29 March 1699 the north-west corner of the north transept collapsed. Dean Lambe had to mount a fund-raising campaign. The chapter had decided that it should be built 'exactly in the manner and on the same foundations as it stood before' *(Fig. 12)*. This was a rather remarkable decision for its date and required the careful copying of all the Romanesque detail as well as the gothic windows. It was undertaken by Robert Grumbold, a skilful mason who carried out Wren's plans in the great new library at Trinity College, Cambridge. Lambe cast his fund-raising net wide and was told by Archbishop Tenison, who had agreed to help, to consult Christopher Wren and report back to him.

Wren's view of the cause of the collapse (based on the dean's description) was that the northernmost pier had given way, because it had fallen inwards. He and Simon ffulkes (his chief mason at St Paul's) had some difficulty in understanding Grumbold's plan, but suggested that the dean and chapter were being overcharged. Wren advocated the use of new stone only for the window surrounds but said that 'good old stone is as good as new, for all other uses'. He assured the dean that the work could be finished in two summers, in which time 'the builder will find no decay in his scaffolding'.

Grumbold wanted to case the outside in new stone and seems to have prevailed even though ffulkes advised that this would be 'neither strength nor ornament because it will be unlike the rest'.

Simon ffulkes was, however, insistent that the builders should 'put on the same cap ... that was upon it before, for it is not an ornament only, but a mighty strength, even as good as a Buttress by reason of its weight'. He was evidently referring to the conical top of the big corner turret, which would divert the lateral thrust of the transept arcade down into the foundations. A few contemporary details were introduced, especially the handsome north door which Grumbold seems to have copied from Wren's door at St Mary-le-Bow, and the window above it which comes straight from his Trinity College library. But there is no direct evidence that Wren himself came to Ely or took a hand in the design. The repairs were complete in 1702. The lantern leadwork was repaired in 1707, and in 1709 Grumbold was asked to look at the condition of the south transept and built the great buttress which houses the south entrance.

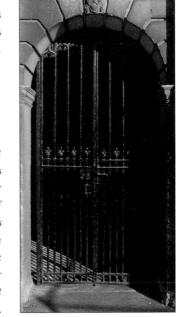

*89. Robert Grumbold's south door encloses a pair of medieval gates which were given by Bishop Alcock (1486–1500) for another context (see pp. **97–98**).*

10. The Eighteenth Century

The first half of the eighteenth century is uneventful but in 1757 the architect James Essex is employed to report on necessary repairs. He saves the lantern and the presbytery gable from collapse. His interest in medieval architecture complements that of the canon, James Bentham, whose history published in 1771 is a landmark in early cathedral studies. Its plates announce the dramatic reordering of the east end in which Alan of Walsingham's stalls are moved into the presbytery and the pulpitum is destroyed.

In the early eighteenth century the desire of the established Church to steer a steady course between the twin evils of reforming 'enthusiasm' and Catholic 'superstition' left very few marks on the building. Daniel Defoe made a fleeting, foggy visit to Ely in 1722 when the 'Isle of Ely looked as if wrapped up in blankets and nothing to be seen, but now and then the lanthorn or cupola of Ely Minster'. In spite of the late seventeenth-century repairs it was the poor condition of the cathedral that impressed him but this was clearly a second-hand opinion. By this time, however, there is little evidence that repair work was continuing.

The monuments of the eighteenth-century bishops are models of restraint in which traditional Christian symbols are eschewed in favour of a display of classical propriety *(Fig. 90)*. Few of them have effigies and the vertical format, within which each is a learned variant of its predecessor, arises from their original placing against the eastern piers of Northwold's presbytery. In this they were following the example

of Dean Caesar, whose monument in 1636 was originally placed against one of Hotham's piers. So this area of the church, where Etheldreda's shrine had once attracted the burials of the medieval bishops, continued to function as a mausoleum of the great and the good.

James Bentham

It was not until the middle of the century that serious thought was given again to the repair of the building. It is at this period that we can detect the beginnings of a scholarly interest in its architectural development. James Bentham,

90. Elegant variations on a theme (opposite and overleaf): the monuments of three eighteenth-century bishops: (right) Bishop John Moore (died 1714); (overleaf, left) Bishop William Fleetwood (died 1723), by E. Stanton and C. Horsenail; (overleaf, right) Bishop Thomas Greene (died 1738).

who was admitted to the foundation as a minor canon in 1736, wrote what is perhaps the best cathedral history of the eighteenth century. His research for *The History and Antiquities of the Conventual and Cathedral Church of Ely* was well under way by 1756 and the great work was published in 1771, eight years before he was finally given one of the prebendal stalls. The book is remarkable for its careful and reliable historical research. Bentham, who was in touch with the leading antiquaries of his time, also produced but did not publish an *Account of Saxon, Norman and Gothic Architecture*. This was a pioneer attempt to make some sense of English medieval architecture as a whole and to establish a chronology. If the eighteenth-century

bishops' monuments display a firm grasp of classical design, medieval architecture, by contrast, had become an impenetrable mystery. We might be inclined to smile at Bentham's suggestion that the late twelfth-century infirmary is probably the Saxon church. But we have to remember that he had no works of reference and could not travel easily to see comparable buildings.

Repairs in the mid-eighteenth century

In 1757 James Essex was invited at Bentham's instigation to make a report on the fabric. Essex was a sensitive architect and in the courts of the Cambridge colleges his additions and alterations blend well with their surroundings. He assisted Bentham with the development of his ideas on historic styles and set about a wide-ranging and very necessary repair of the cathedral. The eastern gable of the presbytery was 60 centimetres out of plumb and its correction was one of the projects of the first year. So was the repair and alteration of the lantern, whose timbers had been badly weakened by rot and death-watch beetle. But whereas the 1707 work had conserved much of the medieval form and detail, Essex appears to have embarked on a radical simplification which left the lantern looking like a large gothick garden pavilion. The flying buttresses were stripped away, the diagonally set angle turrets were rebuilt square and the windows were given tracery of the most basic kind. The sound carpentry of Essex did, however, save the lantern from a worse fate. In 1762 the Galilee porch, whose demolition Essex had advocated, was repaired and in 1768 the thirteenth-century timber roof of the eastern arm was completely replaced *(Fig. 91)*.

It was in this year that it was finally decided to move the choir into the presbytery. This scheme, first hatched by Bishop Gunning, had received enthusiastic support from Browne Willis in his account of Ely first published in 1730. St Paul's cathedral had come to epitomise the glories of the established Church. Willis saw, in its huge centralised crossing and dome, an effect that might be achieved by the medieval architecture of Ely if only the stalls could be moved. Bentham and Essex made up for lost time in the great removal operation of 1770–1. The stalls were moved into Northwold's presbytery *(Fig. 92)*, where their introduction damaged the medieval monuments against which they were placed. As Thomas Cocke has made clear, this damage was the responsibility of Bentham and the chapter rather than Essex. The centre was cut out of Bishop de Luda's tomb to turn it into a choir entrance *(Fig. 51)*. Essex had already experimented with this con-

91. The new pine roof of the choir, built by James Essex in 1768, pays tribute to its thirteenth-century predecessor in the scissor braces above the upper tie beams.

figuration in a De Luda-style garden gate for Horace Walpole at Strawberry Hill in 1769. Part of the bishop's tomb chest was now used to create a new receptacle for the bones of the Saxon benefactors in the chapel of Bishop West. The stone screen beneath which they were originally enshrined in the octagon was demolished and its remarkable wall paintings lost for ever. Many of Essex and Bentham's interventions were urgent and saved the building from disaster, but the baffling trail of incidental damage shows an attitude of mind as remote from our own time as the Middle Ages were from them. It has to be remembered however that at this period very few people in England took a serious interest in

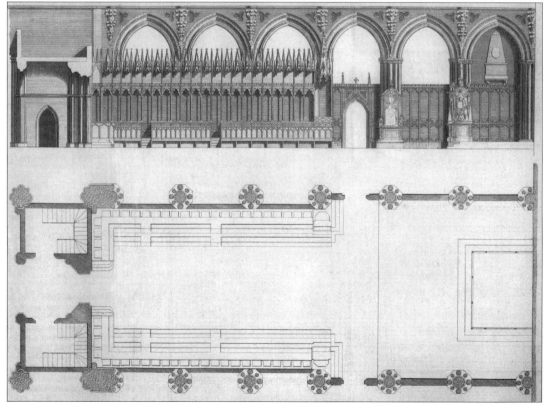

the preservation of medieval antiquities for their own sake. The presbytery of Bishop Northwold had become redundant. Bentham and his contemporaries associated its former use with superstitious practices that had no place in the rational religion of their time. So the creative effort put into the repair and refurnishing of this area in a sympathetic manner, as the setting for daily worship, was in many ways an enlightened attempt to adapt the cathedral for modern requirements. The work was completed with some new stained glass for the east window. It was painted by James Pearson on the basis of an agreement of 1769 and paid for by Bishop Mawson. It was intended to be quite an elaborate composition filling the three great lancets, incorporating coats of arms and a nativity with figures of saints including the evangelists, Etheldreda, Peter and Paul, but it was never finished. St Peter's figure alone remains in the cathedral, in one of the windows of the north nave tribune where it is accompanied by some of the coats of arms *(Col. pl. 17)*. The rich and well-chosen colours combined with strong modelling show what a fine window this might have been.

93. James Bentham (1708–94), from an engraving after T. Kerrich.

92. (left) Illustrations from James Bentham's The History and Antiquities of the Conventual and Cathedral Church of Ely. *(top left) The octagon and lantern before Essex's alterations. (top right) The octagon and lantern as Essex intended them (the lower pinnacles were not, however, completed). (bottom) Plan and elevation made to illustrate the proposed removal of the choir to the east end of the presbytery in 1771 (from the second edition, 1812). Notice the monuments of Bishops Moore and Patrick in their original positions against Northwold's piers.*

11. The Nineteenth Century

This is one of the liveliest periods in the history of the cathedral. The repairs and alterations of earlier years are superseded by the more ambitious projects of the Victorian revival. Dean Peacock begins the restoration with the repair of the south-west transept in 1844 and then employs Gilbert Scott to move the choir stalls once more. The operation is complete by 1852. Scott restores the lantern to its medieval form and remarkable painted ceilings, undertaken between 1858 and 1878, enrich the interior. Ely acquires an unrivalled collection of Victorian stained glass.

Romantic decline

It was not long before the excellent engravings of Bentham's history began to feed the imaginations of contemporary architects. Their clients had for some years demanded new buildings in the gothic taste. In 1782 James Wyatt designed, at Lee priory in Kent, a little gothick library with a vaulted ceiling and a central lantern in imitation of the octagon. It was the forerunner of the much more spectacular Fonthill, which Wyatt began for William Beckford in 1796, two years after he had been called in at Ely to advise on the west tower. The plan was cruciform as at Lee priory and the wings radiated from a lofty central octagon and lantern – a confection of plaster and timber – which was to collapse in 1825.

It was in about 1796 that Turner, who was later to paint views of Fonthill, visited Ely and made the drawings for his astonishing watercolour of the octagon *(Col. pl. 14)*. In this painting and in Fonthill are many of the ingredients

of the early Romantic Movement. There is feeling for the grandeur and inaccessibility of the remote past, a sense of theatre and a certain *laissez-faire* about points of detail and structure, both architectural and pictorial. Much of the work done about the cathedral in the following years was to have a theatrical and cosmetic quality.

In 1802 the conclusion of a temporary peace with France was celebrated by hoisting a crown of candles into the lantern to illuminate it for those outside. Fortunately the resulting fire was extinguished by the prompt action of a workman who hacked out the burning timbers. In the same year Essex's choir was given an altarpiece with an appropriate subject, a version of the dramatic painting by Ribera of *St Peter's Release from Prison*.

The west end

The main attention in 1802 was, however, focused on the west end where the stuccoist Francis Bernasconi repaired the Galilee. In the

Plate 11. Panels illustrating scenes from the life of Etheldreda. They were discovered serving as cupboard doors in an Ely cottage by James Bentham in the 1780s. Dendrochronology has dated them to 1445–60. In 1455 Brother John of Soham, who was in charge of the shrine of Etheldreda, listed payments to Robert Pygot, the painter of Bury St Edmunds, in connection with a new canopy. The style has been compared with a manuscript Life of St Edmund and St Fremund made at Bury c.1430 (British Library, MS Harley 2278). These paintings, which may have been made for the reredos of the shrine altar, show Etheldreda's marriage to Ecgfrid (top left); her parting with Ecgfrid (top right); the saint overseeing the building of her church at Ely (bottom left); the first translation of Etheldreda (bottom right; one of the nuns points to the place on her neck where the swelling has subsided). The church building scene shows fifteenth-century masons with their axes and chisels. The mason in the foreground uses the characteristic L-shaped square to establish the correct angle on his block. Mortar is being distributed in wicker baskets. The inscriptions beneath each scene come from a late thirteenth- or early fourteenth-century Ely manuscript (British Library, MS Cotton, Domitian xv) and are evidently descriptions of an earlier image cycle. (Society of Antiquaries of London)

Plate 12. North transept, hammer-beam roof (c.1430).

Plate 13. (above) The effigy of Sir Robert Steward (died 1570). (below) The funeral of Bishop Cox in 1581. This is the earliest post-Reformation painting of a known church interior and shows the original arrangement of the monks' choir in the octagon. The whole composition is reversed. (right) The monument of Henry Caesar (dean 1614–36). The superscription is 'calm after the storm'.

Plate 14. (left) The octagon and choir in c.1796: watercolour by J.M.W. Turner. The effect of Essex and Bentham's reordering can be appreciated. The late seventeenth-century organ case stands on Essex's screen. His tracery fills the windows of the lantern. It is Sunday morning and the congregation is attending to a sermon which is being preached from a pulpit on the extreme right. (City of Aberdeen, Art Gallery and Museums Collections)

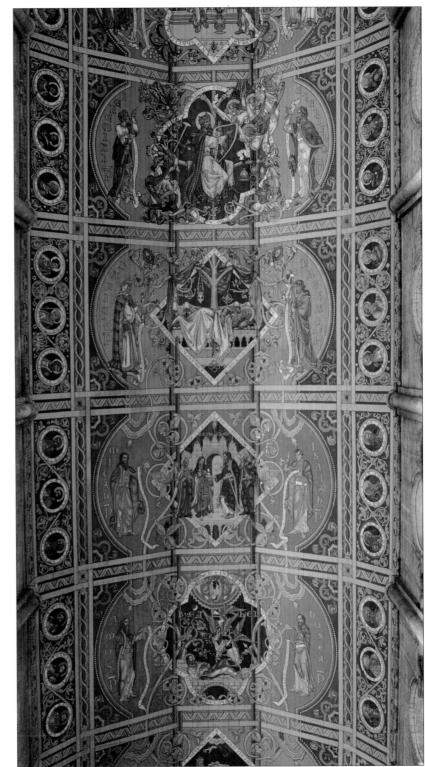

Plate 15. (right) The nave ceiling (1861–4). Henry le Strange's work is below and the more colourful and ambitious painting of Thomas Gambier Parry above. Le Strange has given the figure of Isaiah the features of Dean Peacock. (centre, right)

Plate 16. Victorian stained glass. (above) Three scenes from the life of Samson, by Alfred Gérente. This window was shown at the Great Exhibition of 1851. (above right) Peter and other disciples meet Jesus by the lake of Tiberius after the Resurrection, by Clayton & Bell, 1860. (right) The Healing Miracles of Christ by Henry Holiday for Powells of Whitefriars, after 1891. (far right) Bishops Balsham and Hotham by Clayton & Bell, 1900.

Plate 17. (left) St Peter from James Pearson's glass, commissioned for the east window of the presbytery in 1769.

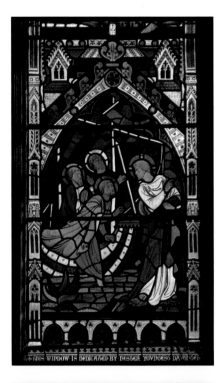

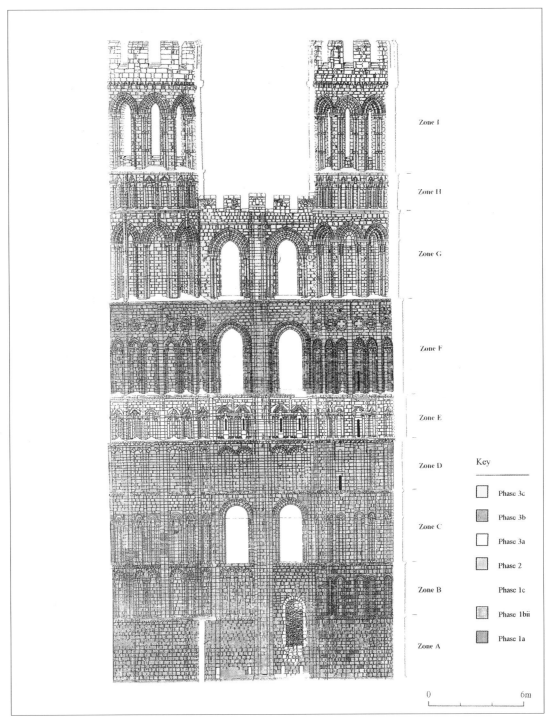

Plate 18. A drawing from K. Fearn, P. Marshall and G. Simpson 'The South-west Transept of Ely Cathedral', 1995, illustrating the different campaigns of stone-laying in which the transept was built. Archaeologists are now applying to standing structures the analytical methods hitherto associated with excavation.

THE LITTLEPORT RIOTS

Agricultural depression in the years following the Napoleonic wars led to widespread rural deprivation and civil unrest. In 1816 rioting and looting broke out in nearby Littleport. A large crowd armed with guns and agricultural implements made their way to Ely where they damaged some houses and shops. The bishop still held his time-honoured jurisdiction over the Isle of Ely and the canons sat as justices of the peace. After the arrest of eighty rioters a variety of exemplary sentences were handed down. Five men were condemned to death and five to transportation. The trials followed a service in the cathedral at which the preacher was a newly appointed canon, Sir Henry Bate Dudley. His youthful dissipation had been followed by a career in journalism, which he combined with a comfortable clerical life. The riots provided a perfect opportunity for his excitable and theatrical temperament. He had ridden as a justice of the peace at the head of the cavalry that rooted out the offenders from their hiding places in the fen. Now he preached from Paul's first letter to Timothy ('law is not made for a righteous man, but for the lawless and unruly, for the ungodly and sinners, for the unholy and profane'). It was not the first time in its history that the cathedral was associated with the repression of the local population by a privileged elite.

was built above the western crossing – inspired, no doubt, by the obvious signs that a stone vault was intended in the fifteenth-century alterations. Bernasconi was employed again in 1823 to undertake repairs and to paint large areas of the church in yellow, ochre and white. In the Lady chapel the parish undertook a less successful amateur version of this treatment with their own resources.

Bernasconi's men are reputed to have taken fragments of remaining medieval glass from the cathedral windows during repairs. They were later returned, but much greater quantities had probably been lost in the repair works of the eighteenth century. Numerous pieces were to be found lying in the earth between the Lady chapel buttresses and local children used the deep colours to view solar eclipses. The stirrings of a revival of interest in ancient glass are marked at Ely by Bishop Yorke's gift, in 1807, of a new west window. Its glazing is a collection of sixteenth-century continental glass, which was cleverly extended by Charles Clutterbuck in 1853. This window was introduced to replace the blocking of the western arch, carried out when the roof was taken off the Galilee. The next generation was to judge the work of these years harshly and our own view of it is perhaps unduly influenced by the polemical outbursts that fired the Victorian revival.

COBBETT: A DECAYING BUILDING AND THE NEGLECT OF THE POOR

It was around the year 1830 that Ely came to the attention of three men who were to have a remarkable effect on its future. William Cobbett, whose *Rural Rides* are a panoramic depiction of England on the edge of the Victorian age, visited Ely on 28 March 1830. Twenty-one years earlier he had been given a two-year gaol sentence and a £1,000 fine for criticising the government over an incident in

outer arch he removed the low, late medieval openings, remodelling the head of the door with a flowing tracery design *(Fig. 102)* and carrying out similar changes to the inner door. Much of this was of Roman cement, a patent composition stone much used at this period. It has lasted surprisingly well. The main arches of the western crossing had all been closed up in the previous century. Now the great arch to the nave was reopened. A timber and plaster vault which the mutinous Ely militia were brutally disciplined by four squadrons of German cavalry from Ipswich. He had now come to the cathedral city with a view to 'haranguing' the local people on the social ills of contemporary England.

> Arrived at Ely, I first walked round the beautiful Cathedral, that honour to our Catholic forefathers, and that standing disgrace to our Protestant selves. It is impossible to look at that magnificent pile without *feeling* that we are a fallen race of men … They say that the bishop has an income of £18,000 a year. He and the dean and chapter are the owners of all the land and tithes for a great distance round about in this beautiful and most productive part of the country; and yet this famous building, the cathedral is in a state of disgraceful irrepair and disfigurement. The great and magnificent windows to the east have been shortened at the bottom, and the space plastered up with brick and mortar, in a very slovenly manner, for the purpose of saving the expense of keeping the glass in repair … And the churchyard contained a flock of sheep acting as vergers for those who live upon the immense income, not a penny of which ought to be expended upon themselves while any part of this beautiful building is in a state of irrepair.

That evening, Cobbett went to an inn that overlooked the Market Place and addressed the local farmers in a small and ill-ventilated room. Pointing towards the cathedral he demanded:

> Can you believe, gentlemen, that when that magnificent pile was reared, and when all the fine monasteries, hospitals, schools, and other resorts of piety and charity existed in this town and neighbourhood; can you believe that Ely was the miserable little place that it is now; and that England which had never heard of the name *pauper* contained the crowds of miserable creatures that it now contains, some starving at stone-cracking by

the wayside and others drawing loaded waggons on that way?

Cobbett's *History of the Protestant Reformation*, which had been published in 1824–7, coincided with the emancipation of the English Catholics who, since the reign of Elizabeth, had lived under a series of harsh penalties and restrictions. The book sold 40,000 copies and was undoubtedly crucial in forming the views of the brilliant architect, designer and evangelist of the gothic revival, A.W.N. Pugin.

PUGIN: CHRISTIAN ARCHITECTURE

On walking into the Lady chapel, which was then cluttered with the cheap box pews and smothered in thick coats of limewash, Pugin is reputed to have burst into tears and exclaimed, 'O God, what has England done to deserve this.' In 1836 he published *Contrasts or a Parallel between the Noble Edifices of the Middle Ages and the Corresponding Buildings of the Present Day, Showing the Present Decay of Taste*. It changed the way that a whole generation thought about architecture. In a series of very clever and scurrilous comparative illustrations he argued that since the Middle Ages architecture had fallen into a decline and was now virtually bankrupt. A number of the drawings illustrate the points made by Cobbett. One, for example, shows the beautiful almshouses of the fifteenth century contrasted with a prison-like Poor Law union building of his own time. If Cobbett had made a connection between the morality of the Church and the decline of its ancient buildings, Pugin went further. 'Pointed or Christian Architecture', he wrote, 'has far higher claims to our admiration than beauty or antiquity … in it alone we find *the faith of Christianity embodied and its practices illustrated.*' Pugin meant that churches built in the form of a cross signified the Crucifixion, that the triangular forms of gothic arches depicted the Trinity, and the aspiring lines of a gothic building symbolised the Resurrection.

The third notable early nineteenth-century visitor to Ely was George Gilbert Scott. He first saw the cathedral as a youth while staying with his elder brother at Cambridge in 1828. He was about to embark on a career in architecture and sought out medieval buildings to sketch. He did not know that he was to begin in a dreary but profitable practice designing the grim Poor Law union buildings in which rural society's most vulnerable members were incarcerated. In the early 1840s, however, Scott discovered Pugin.

Pugin's articles excited me almost to a fury and I suddenly found myself like a person awakened from a long feverish dream which rendered him unconscious of what was going on about him … A new phase had come over me, thoroughly *en rapport* with my earlier taste, but in utter discord with the 'fitful fever' of my poor law activity.

Restoration

To these new men of the early Victorian age the architecture of the cathedral, and of all ancient churches, now mattered in a way that it had not done since the convulsions of the Reformation. Building was once more a moral issue. Everyone at Ely, from the dean to the craftsmen, seems to have been aware of the distinction, both ethical and technical, between their endeavours and the work of the early nineteenth century. Certainly John Bacon, the clerk of works, was in no doubt about the moral inferiority of the early nineteenth-century work.

Lath and plaster moulded into incongruous forms, hid from view works of great merit and beauty; yellow ochre, white and stone colored wash covered alike the mottled clunch, the grey marble and the mellow stone wrought into

enchanting forms; the contrast of color [*sic*] was as if between the emblems of sin and purity; yellow and white.

Bacon's careful manuscript record of all the nineteenth-century work also signifies intense pride and commitment. In 1839 a new dean was installed at Ely. George Peacock was one of the most brilliant mathematicians of his generation and a mover and shaker in the University of Cambridge. There he was involved in a series of architectural projects including the Observatory, the new University Library, the University Press and the Fitzwilliam Museum, the classical masterpiece of the architect George Basevi. He would also have been immersed in the new enthusiasm for the proper understanding and 'correct' restoration of medieval churches which led to the foundation of the Cambridge Camden Society in the year of his installation as dean. Peacock's first priority at Ely was to improve the setting of the cathedral. He converted a series of fields which occupied the site of Alan of Walsingham's vineyard and the earthworks of the old castle into a very beautiful informal landscape park. It was one of Peacock's many gifts to posterity, and with the young trees in place he turned his mind to the cathedral itself.

Peacock found himself among a group of canons whose enthusiasm for medieval antiquities and the work of restoration rivalled his own. When he proposed to remove a single Romanesque capital from the old monastic kitchen (so that the deanery drawing room could have a window looking onto the cathedral) they rose in revolt. He backed down, remarking that 'the cackling of the geese saved the capitol'. Two members of the Ely clergy were to be particularly significant. One was Canon Edward Bowyer Sparke, the son of the former bishop. He managed the fund which he established with his father and brother to pay for a good deal of the Victorian stained glass and contributed a number of windows and other important furnishings himself. Another was David Stewart, the minor canon whose *Architectural History of Ely Cathedral* published in 1868 remains a very valuable account of the building and of the monastery.

Nearly all the work undertaken by the Victorians at Ely was informed by careful archaeological investigation and historical research. Robert Willis, Jacksonian professor at Cambridge and the father of cathedral archaeology, was a close friend of Peacock. When the dean and chapter committed the last act of post-Reformation vandalism with the demolition, in 1843, of the magnificent Sextry barn, Willis recorded its structure with exemplary care. In mitigation, there rose on its site a group of neo-Tudor almshouses. They were designed by Basevi and funded by the fifteenth-century charity of Thomas Parsons, of which the dean was a governor.

In the following year Willis began to work with Peacock on the opening up and restoration of the south-west transept, made possible by a donation from Edward Sparke. This, the most ornate part of the Romanesque cathedral, had become a workshop and was both disfigured and decaying. Only recently has archaeological work revealed the very extensive internal stonework repairs to its interior undertaken at this time. The three adjacent arches of the south nave aisle had also been completely blocked with about 2 metres of rubble and were now reopened. Repairs were made to the lead roofs and the west tower received attention. It was continuing to move in a rather alarming fashion. Workmen taking out floor timbers in 1845 panicked when a part-sawn beam snapped with a loud report and moved over 2 centimetres apart. It was during these repairs that Basevi, who was being shown round, stepped through a gap in the floor and tragically fell to his death 9 metres below in one of the pockets of the lath and plaster vault.

Moving the choir

In 1844 Peacock and Willis had begun to take down Essex's screen at the east end of the choir. This allowed the restoration of Bishop Alcock's chapel (financed by the master and fellows of Jesus College) and the repair of the interior of Northwold's presbytery and of Hotham's work. Two years later, in 1846, the chapter discussed a plan to move the choir and its furnishings again. It would involve much disruption and the destruction of Essex's organ screen, so it was important to obtain the services of an architect who could knit the whole design together in a convincing manner.

In 1847 Gilbert Scott, then enjoying a holiday in the Lake District, received the invitation to mastermind this operation. He had come to international prominence by winning, in 1844, the competition to design the new Nikolai Kirche in Hamburg. Ely was, however, the beginning of his remarkable career as a cathedral restorer. He learnt much from his association with Dean Peacock, whom he regarded as his dear friend and 'one of the noblest of men'. Until this time Scott had believed that the gothic style had originated in Germany; it was only after Peacock had advised him to visit Chartres and Amiens that he discovered that its true origins were French. He was a fast learner. Travelling by rail, he built up a prodigious practice and quickly amassed a formidable knowledge of medieval architecture.

In the new arrangement the choir was to fill the three bays built by Bishop Hotham. This had obvious advantages. It opened up the full

94. (right) Gilbert Scott's reordering of the choir (completed in 1852) was executed with characteristic Victorian self-confidence and conviction. Handsome marble and tile pavements like this one were to feature in all his later cathedral schemes. The organ case was inspired by the one at Strasbourg. (Photograph by Philip Dixon)

95. The delicate iron tracery of Scott's screen to the south choir aisle was made by Skidmore of Coventry in 1856.

six bays of Northwold's presbytery. It allowed the repair of the monuments, which had been badly damaged in the eighteenth-century move, and it was as near as was possible to the medieval arrangement without infringing the uncluttered volume of the octagon. There was a surprising unanimity that Alan of Walsingham's layout should not be re-created. Throughout his work at Ely, and elsewhere, Scott had the Cambridge Camden Society looking over his shoulder, and publishing its approbation and disdain in the *Ecclesiologist*. In 1847 the journal fired a warning shot:

> there would be great objection to replacing the choir in the lantern, when once it had been removed from that noble area. The course would

therefore be to place a light screen across the east end of the lantern and fix the stalls in [Hotham's] Middle Pointed bays.

As Scott was later to write: 'So imperious was their law, that anyone who dared to deviate from or to build in other than the sacred "Middle Pointed", well knew what he must suffer.'

There would also have been considerable local objection to the blocking of the octagon. Churchgoing Ely society would assemble here on Sunday mornings, after parish services around the town, to hear the sermon that followed morning prayer *(Col. pl. 14)*. Beforehand the professional gentlemen paraded in the transepts and octagon while others walked up and down the nave aisles in small groups.

Bacon has given us a vivid picture of this carefully segregated event:

> As soon as the organist began to play, all the congregation took their seats, the canon came from his vestry to the pulpit, the Bishop came out of the choir and took his chair, one of the lay clerks gave out a Hymn from the organ loft, after which the sermon was preached ... The congregation at the sermon comprised the Bishop and Clergy, who were seated on a raised dais under the organ-gallery on the south side; the Gentry sat on the north side, the farmers and tradesmen were seated below the dais round the pulpit, ... The Free School boys (Mrs Needham's Charity) ... were placed in the north aisle, as well as the national School girls ..., the Poor and the Paupers of the Parish sat on forms placed under the octagon, towards the nave on the west side of the passage left for the gentlemen to parade from transept to transept ... Each family had to provide a seat or bench; ... they were not confined to uniformity either of make, material or colour ... – these seats with their foot boards were removed every Monday morning into the aisle and set out again on Saturday for the Sunday sermon by the Vergers

The re-creation of the fourteenth-century layout would have completely changed this long-established usage.

In the eighteenth-century choir of Essex the clergy had enjoyed a rather private, collegiate service behind his substantial organ screen. It is noticeable that all Scott's great cathedral screens are transparent, enabling a larger congregation to see and hear the choir service. Ely was the forerunner and visibility necessitated the removal of some of the return stalls at the west end to create this effect. The screen was built in timber and in its freedom from exact precedent shows Scott's ability to design in gothic as though it were a living style still capable of development. The contractor for the whole project was James Rattee, who produced carved woodwork of first-rate quality for the screen and for the sub-stalls whose ends were decorated with a series of impressive figures carved by J.B. Philip. The great brass gates were made by John Hardman of Birmingham and the figure sculpture of the screen is by M. Abeloos of Louvain.

It was the sort of screen that the *Ecclesiologist* wanted but they found it a little too rich for the comparatively restrained medieval stalls. Phillip Lindley has suggested very plausibly that the introduction of sculpted reliefs beneath each stall canopy was a response to this criticism. A sample panel was provided by J.B. Philip but Abeloos carved the rest, with Old Testament scenes on the south and a gospel narrative on

96. The balustrade of Gilbert Scott's pulpit (1866), by Potters of South Moulton Street.

127

97. A Gurney stove. The cathedral was so cold in the winter that the thirteenth-century monks were given a special dispensation to wear caps in the choir. By 1852 the choir was heated. The much-loved Gurney stoves were introduced to warm the congregation in 1867 and are now the sole source of heat in the winter months.

French gothic. The use of foreign styles distinguished the Victorian revival from the early nineteenth century. In the previous year work had begun on a remarkable altar screen and reredos at the east end *(Col. pl. 5)*. The reredos is an exceptionally rich confection in Italian gothic, housing a series of reliefs inspired by the paintings of Giotto and Fra Angelico. These are set behind mosaic-encrusted, spiral pillars supporting canopies like those of the Scala family tombs in Verona.

Scott visited Italy for the first time in 1851 and, summarising his impressions much later, wrote, 'I was convinced … that Italian Gothic as such, must not be used in England, but I was equally convinced, and am so still, that the study of it is necessary to the perfection of the revival.' The reliefs were by Philip, and the fading painted decoration represents hours of labour by the over-sensitive Octavius Hudson, who set to work only when the spirit moved him. He once put down his brushes and returned to London when he overheard the adverse comment of a tourist. Although the painting was not finished before 1868, the choir was opened for worship in 1852. Warmed by pipes hidden beneath the medieval stalls, and surrounded by a bravura display of neo-gothic carving, the clergy and choir found themselves in a setting of great comfort and magnificence.

Painted ceilings

In 1855 Henry Styleman le Strange began the painting of the west tower ceiling which, together with the lantern beneath, had been revealed by the removal of the plaster vault. The Victorian painted ceilings at Ely are very ambitious and extensive. They were only possible because Le Strange and his successor were men of private means who gave their services gratis. In 1858 the thirteenth-century timbers of the nave roof were hidden for the first time in six hundred years by a covering of boards imported

the north. In 1850 the white and yellow wash was cleaned off the octagon, revealing for the first time the outlines of tracery patterns on the webs of the timber vault.

In 1851 Rattee built a great new organ case which Scott had designed on the model of one at Strasbourg, crowned with an orchestra of trumpeting angels. Its function was mainly decorative; nearly all the mechanism and pipes of the much extended and augmented organ were laid out in the gallery behind. The case did however conceal the organ loft for which Scott designed a delightful spiral staircase in late from St Petersburg. Le Strange continued his work with the painting of the roof in the south gallery of Hotham's choir in 1860 and in the following year he began work on the new nave ceiling *(Col. pl. 15)*.

His method was to make a small study for each section, 15–20 centimetres across, and then to transfer this by squaring to pieces of paper the full size of the final design. Other sheets of paper, which had previously been coated with red ochre, were placed against the whitened ceiling boards and the full-scale cartoons pinned over them. The painter's boy then went over each line with a metal point and this transferred a thin red outline of the designs to the boards. The painting was then undertaken. Le Strange was most anxious that the work should not be too bright and would constantly require the scaffold boards to be removed so that he could judge the effect from the ground and then tone it down. He was a self-effacing and scholarly artist who based his design on late twelfth-century sources: stained-glass windows at Chartres and the dancing, attenuated figure style of the famous Winchester Psalter. This was one of the manuscripts which he carefully copied during many hours of study in the British Museum. After a few months, much to the consternation of the dean and chapter, Le Strange went off to work at St Albans, Holborn, for his friend the architect William Butterfield. He became ill and died shortly afterwards.

Fortunately, his fellow Etonian Thomas Gambier Parry was prepared to complete the work as a memorial to his fellow artist at no charge. Working with the two assistants trained by Le Strange, Parry finished the ceiling in time for Christmas 1864. He was worried that the egg tempera technique used by Le Strange would not last and he did not approve of the low tonal range in which the work was executed. He also felt that his friend had stuck too closely to his medieval sources. Parry, like many artists at the time, was anxious not simply to revive a dead style but to develop it into a living tradition. His eastern half of the ceiling was executed in his own 'Ely medium' of drying oil, copal varnish and japanner's gold size, and his colours are considerably brighter. The figures are solidly depicted with greater naturalism and the scenes are altogether more complex.

The restoration of the lantern

In the last panel of Le Strange's work the figure of Isaiah is a portrait of Dean Peacock, who had died in 1858. The promoter of the nave ceiling decoration was the new dean, Harvey Goodwin, whose unfinished memoir of his time at Ely is an entertaining account of these eventful years at the cathedral. His greatest achievement was the restoration of the octagon lantern, as a memorial to Peacock. This project was launched in 1859:

> Eventually we instructed Scott to give us a design for the restoration of the lantern. Somewhat to our surprise, he sent us down, without special examination of the structure, a smart looking drawing of the lantern, as he proposed that it should be. If my memory does not deceive me, we lithographed the drawing, for use as a kind of begging circular, but it was of no value whatever as an architectural design.

By this stage Scott's practice had become very busy indeed. He had a large office and was at work in every corner of the country. Le Strange, who had taken a hand in some of the architectural design for alterations at the deanery, had formed the view that the belfry of the lantern was a later addition and that there had once been a spire. Scott listened attentively to his argument and then asked to be left alone in the belfry with a carpenter. An hour later he emerged with conclusive evidence that the belfry was original. In spite of the false start represented by the 'smart looking drawing',

Scott's final restoration, guided by eighteenth-century prints and his careful examination of the structure, has been shown by Lindley to be a broadly reliable reconstruction of Hurley's masterpiece.

The internal decoration of the vault and lantern, by contrast, was an entirely Victorian invention. Octavius Hudson, who had repainted the medieval polychrome of the adjacent transept roofs, made an investigation of the original evidence in 1868. In the same year the artist and stained-glass designer C.E. Kempe produced a scheme that promised to restore many of its features. Gambier Parry somehow managed to get the job, however, and his scheme was executed in green and gold with lilies, crowns and, in the lantern, a group of boldly coloured angels. It resembles contemporary 'aesthetic' fashion but a few medieval rood lofts retain rather similar decoration in the webs of their miniature timber vaults. A passage in the manuscript of Scott's posthumous *Personal and Professional Recollections* excised by the editor shows that Gambier Parry, having devised the lantern decoration without consulting the architect, had actually asked the dean and chapter to cut him out of the discussions. This they would not do, but Scott, who habitually expressed himself with diffidence, did not stand in his way. He wrote, however, 'he has followed his own devices and neglected all the evidence of ancient decoration though not wholly unsuccessful in his result'.

In 1878 Gambier Parry completed his work at Ely with a handsome ceiling over the south-west transept. These great fields of colour add greatly to the richness of the cathedral without detracting from the austere grandeur of the Romanesque architecture. Fortunately Le Strange never carried out his scheme to add colour to the stonework of the nave itself, though Gambier Parry seems to have painted the upper arches of the octagon and the tracery of the windows. All this work was soon to come under fire from William Morris and others. They felt that in their decayed and neglected state these buildings had great qualities which the work of restoration destroyed. In a letter of 1879 to William Bryce (an early member of the Society for the Protection of Ancient Buildings which Morris founded), Morris wrote:

> Ely you must have seen; I never saw it before it had been daubed over like a music hall; but what it must have looked, the rich choir the amazing lantern & that finest of all Norman naves – what they must have looked when they were all grey & venerable together I can partly imagine: I hear they threaten the ... Lady Chapel now.

Morris's fierce attacks on Scott and others were instrumental in turning public opinion against Victorian church restorations. The work of Scott and his contemporaries has only recently recovered from more than half a century of vilification. Now we can look more objectively at its contribution. Pugin had written of his hope that 'by encouraging talent where it is to be found [they might] raise up ... a race of artists, who could be found able to conceive and execute things equally fine and masterly as in the ancient days'. It cannot be denied that many of the craftsmen who worked in the Victorian restoration of Ely achieved this goal.

In 1856, for example, Scott introduced the beautiful iron screens *(Fig. 95)* which guard the entrances to the choir aisles. Skidmore of Coventry made them and their quality is typical of this very remarkable firm. The framework of each screen is similar but the detail is wonderfully different. Skidmore also made the superb gasoliers or 'coronas' for the choir which Dean Goodwin gave in 1867. In the metal balustrade of the pulpit stairs *(Fig. 96)*, which was made by Potters of South Moulton Street, London, in 1866, not one of the floral bosses is duplicated by another. When Goodwin urged Potter to speed up, he explained 'that he could not put more than one hand upon it as the work of two different hands would not harmonise'. On another occasion during Scott's restoration of the Galilee (1868–70) Dean Goodwin watched one of the carvers at work on the tympanum of the inner door:

> Bernasconi's plaster was replaced by carved work in stone. It was a great pleasure to watch the man who did this work. He was employed by Rattee and Kett of Cambridge. He was a genuine artist, had a true feeling for work, and performed it with wonderful ease. He sat before his sculpture, carving grapes and vine leaves out of his own fancy, with no model, or one of the simplest kind, before him.

STAINED GLASS

Ely illustrates better than any other building the Victorian revival in stained glass. There are more than one hundred windows by most of the significant glass painters of the period. Pearson's powerfully modelled figure of St Peter *(Col. pl. 17)* is an excellent example of glass developed from the contemporary oil-painting tradition. The story of glass painting in the Victorian period is, however, the gradual recovery of the more two-dimensional and linear method of the medieval glaziers. Here clarity of design and subordination to the architectural structure of the window were the key disciplines.

In a window in the north aisle of the nave made in the 1840s by the French glass painter A. Lusson there are scenes from the life of Daniel, grouped within each light under architectural canopies. This work acknowledges the gothic principles of organisation but in a wholly pictorial manner and one would never guess that Lusson had spent much of his time restoring French medieval windows. As the reconstruction of the choir was approaching completion, William Wailes was commissioned to glaze the great lancets of Bishop Northwold's east wall. Thirteenth-century windows of this type were nearly always organised as banks of little scenes inscribed in roundels, lozenges or other more complex, foiled frames. These shapes were formed by stout iron *ferramenta*, which in the case of Ely still survived in the side lancets. These gave Wailes the overall pattern, but he travelled to France to study the windows of Chartres and Bourges to find out how to fill them. The windows, which were made between 1851 and 1857, are very convincing in their overall colour and tonality and probably give a good general idea of the original glazing, but the figure drawing is self-evidently Victorian. This work was paid for by a large legacy from Bishop Sparke which, wisely invested, produced an income from which many other new windows in the cathedral were also financed.

Henri Gérente who had narrowly escaped death by firing squad in the Revolution of 1848, only to die of cholera in 1849, contributed some of the best early Victorian glass in the cathedral. He was succeeded in the work by his younger brother Alfred. In windows like those of the nave south aisle – depicting scenes from the days of Creation and the Fall of Man (1849), and the stories of Noah and of Samson *(Col. pl. 16)* – the Gérentes displayed their remarkable mastery of medieval drawing and design. They chose a late twelfth-century style for these plain Romanesque openings. The *Ecclesiologist*, which reviewed nearly every one of the Ely windows, considered this archaeological style, so close in its approach to the ceilings of Le Strange, to be an artistic cul-de-sac.

An alternative approach is suggested in another window of the south nave aisle, which was designed by A.W.N. Pugin and made in 1852 by John Hardman of Birmingham. It had been remodelled with tracery in the fourteenth century, and this suggested a late gothic glazing scheme with scenes from the life of David under silvery architectural canopies.

There is something harsh about the drawing but the figure groups are powerfully designed and full of energy. The late 1850s saw the rise of Clayton & Bell as a dominant force in Victorian glass painting and Ely has some excellent work by this firm. It fell to them to fill some of the traceried windows of the choir aisles, which they divided, like Pugin's window, into small scenes under canopies. The easternmost window of the south choir aisle is a memorial to Astley Sparke, who was killed in the Charge of the Light Brigade at Balaclava in 1854. It is typical of their strongly architectural work but is excelled in quality by another window by the same firm. This is the memorial to Lieutenant Colonel Pratt of the 17th Lancers (part of the Light Brigade) made in 1860 and showing scenes from the life of St Peter *(Col. pl. 16)*. Here there is a clarity of design and colour which represents High Victorian art at its most appealing and decorative.

After this time Victorian stained glass developed in divergent directions. They are well represented in two other windows. One is Henry Holiday's window made by Powells of Whitefriars after 1891 as a memorial to John Marshall, a past president of the General Medical Council and professor of Anatomy at the Royal Academy of Art *(Col. pl. 16)*. The Healing Miracles of Christ, set against classical architecture and among naturalistically rendered medicinal plants, is the apt subject. The powerful and graceful figures with their classical drapery are combined in a design disciplined by the separate lights of the window without becoming subservient to them in the medieval manner. As early as 1869 Holiday had declared his determination to work in his own manner, whatever the style of the building.

Clayton & Bell's late window of 1900 in Bishop Alcock's chapel *(Col. pl. 16)* could not be more different but this late gothic design is very well suited to its context. The figures of past bishops were drawn by George Daniels, who had

clearly studied the best late gothic art, as well as the work of Holbein and Dürer, to achieve this remarkable level of characterisation and vigour. The architectural surrounds are also beautifully rendered in a restrained palette to create a suave and refined version of English fifteenth-century glass in which the level of illumination is perfectly controlled.

This sort of window was a real fulfilment of Pugin's dream. It shows the persistence of his influence throughout the sixty years of the Victorian revival. In the 1850s and 1860s, under the influence of John Ruskin and G.E. Street, there had been a great deal of experiment with foreign styles, but this hardly touched Ely. The cathedral was evidently regarded as such a valuable document of native architecture that few such liberties could be taken. In the 1870s there was, in any case, a reawakening of interest in English gothic of the late fourteenth and fifteenth centuries and this meant a return to the kind of late medieval buildings which Pugin had illustrated as exemplars.

His drawing entitled 'Contrasted Sepulchral Monuments' *(Fig. 98)* shows a tomb of the 1820s at Salisbury and one of the magnificent fourteenth-century Alard tombs at Winchelsea. The illustrations which follow present a more modern contrast: two Ely tombs, one before and one after the great Victorian restoration. The handsome tomb of Bishop Allen *(Fig. 99)* who died in 1845 represents the last gasp of the early nineteenth-century tradition, and is the sort of eclectic mixture which Pugin abhorred. The architecture has some correct gothic details but they are arranged to fit a standard contemporary monument. The figure of the bishop, moreover, reclining like a Roman dinner guest, his hand extended in an all-encompassing but essentially empty rhetorical gesture, is entirely classical.

The tomb of Bishop Woodford *(Fig. 100)*, who died in 1885, is by contrast a thoroughly convincing essay in late medieval gothic and is the most beautiful Victorian tomb in the cathedral. The alabaster effigy of the bishop, the elaborate canopy and the beautiful iron railings show a complete mastery of the late medieval architectural style. It was designed by G.F. Bodley, the most important church architect of the later nineteenth century, who worked with Pugin's volumes beside him. But this is not to say that the remarkable quality of so much of the Victorian work at Ely is the result of emulating Pugin. His real legacy was the intensity of feeling which motivated these endeavours.

The public interest and acclaim which spurred on artists and architects at Ely to remarkable levels of achievement is reflected in a resolution of the diocesan conference held at Ely in 1874. It called for the establishment of a committee of clergy and laity with branch committees in each archdeaconry to raise funds for the rebuilding of the north-west transept. That no diocesan conference would concern itself with such a matter now is the result of more than a century of changing ideas and two major European wars. The First World War is commemorated at Ely by a fine chapel designed by Guy Dawber in which the names of all the Cambridgeshire dead are recorded. So great is the number that they are painted on folding oak shutters. Dawber made his name as a designer of sensitively understated houses. The joinery of St George's chapel is a restrained late gothic ensemble of considerable subtlety and beauty in which painted decoration is deployed with appropriate decorum. It was completed by 1922.

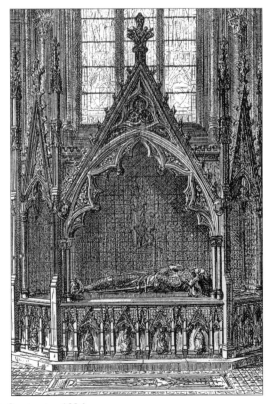

98. 'Contrasted Sepulchral Monuments' from A.W.N. Pugin's Contrasts, *1836.*

99. (above) The monument of Bishop Allen (died 1845), sculpture by I. Ternouth.
100. (right) The monument of Bishop Woodford (died 1885), designed by G.F. Bodley.

12. The Twentieth Century

The twentieth century is a period of consolidation. The effective repair campaigns of the Victorians carry the cathedral into the inter-war years when there are signs of a reaction against the Victorian aesthetic. The beginning of a campaign to remove Victorian glass is halted by the Second World War. Urgent timber repairs begun in the early 1950s become the main preoccupation of the post-war years. Further changes are made in the liturgical arrangements in the 1960s and 1970s. In 1971 work to the west tower initiates the most wide-ranging campaign of repair since the nineteenth century. It continues into the third millennium.

Reacting to the Victorian work

The Victorian belief that gothic could live again, in a reinvigorated Christian culture, began to fall out of step with thinking after the First World War. In the 1920s and 1930s many people found the High Victorian work of Scott and his contemporaries unsympathetic.

At Ely the focus of the reaction was the stained glass. A lecture by Canon E. Milner-White was published in the *Friends of Ely Cathedral Year Book* for 1937. It was 'addressed to a problem which is Ely's above that of any other cathedral except Worcester, the poor quality of the modern glass which, to its grave detriment, fills its windows'. He began by acknowledging that the cathedral was of interest as an unusually complete catalogue of nineteenth-century glass painters. But having established that this interest was historical rather than artistic, he went on to crush some of the lesser efforts with invective worthy of Pugin. Wilmshurst's windows in St Catharine's chapel were 'glass at the lowest and

most degraded moment in its history'. The north nave aisle windows were dismissed one after the other:

> Edgeland, who made 11, is an obscure artist whom I have not met elsewhere, nor want to (or can he be the notorious Hedgeland, who was only stopped in the nick of time from ruining the King's windows?) [he is]. Lusson the Frenchman, we shall speak of later. This window (12) is dreadful

As for the choir aisle windows, he found them mostly of 'indifferent or wretched quality'. One by Lusson on the north side was 'So shocking that it should be removed and destroyed' and an adjacent pair by Ward & Hughes were 'execrable and like Lusson's ought not to deface the Cathedral'. The problem with this cavalier criticism was that by this date only a select few contemporary stained-glass artists could provide convincing work to replace the Victorian windows. In 1938 the dean started the ball rolling by introducing a new window by

Hugh Easton into St Catharine's chapel. Its clear glass surround lets in more light, but the design itself was hardly an encouraging precedent for the future.

The advice on the north nave aisle that 'There is no reason, historical devotional or artistic to be raised on behalf of the retention of these windows' was not taken up. In due course, however, some of the recommendations, particularly in relation to the choir, were adopted. Here interest was first focused on Bishop West's chapel, where a window by Evans of Shrewsbury was to be removed, 'Not only for its own badness but still more because it darkens and conceals the marvellous beauty of the chantry.'

A group formed from the membership of the Theology College, founded by Bishop Woodford in 1881, devoted themselves to the restoration of the chantry, making a start in 1938. Their scheme involved the removal of the glass and the demolition of Bishop Sparke's monument so that an altar could be introduced. The theology students tended to worship at the small church of St Peter on Broad Street whose liturgical tradition was more ritualistic than that of the cathedral. St Peter's has a splendid painted rood screen which is an early work of Ninian Comper, an architect and decorator who worked mainly for Anglo-Catholic clients. Comper was invited to prepare designs for new stained glass and for an altar for the West chantry. The window was later described by Nikolaus Pevsner as 'anaemic' and of the reredos he wrote 'It makes one long for Gilbert Scott.' These contributions were intended to achieve an effect of lightness and delicacy very different from the High Victorian work. A more widespread purge of the cathedral windows was halted by the outbreak of another world war. The war also brought to a premature end Dean Lionel Blackburne's incipient campaign to beautify the cathedral. His foundation of the Friends of Ely Cathedral in 1936, however,

created an organisation that continues to make a substantial contribution to the building, its furnishings and facilities. In 1938, when the Lady chapel was relinquished by the parish of Holy Trinity, its furnishing was one of the Friends' earliest projects.

POST-WAR

The cathedral was lit by gas after the late 1860s. The first experiment with electric light in the cathedral was conducted in 1939 but the war delayed a permanent installation until 1948. In 1949 Stephen Dykes Bower built a new Lady chapel altar but this was the last embellishment for some time. It was now more than a century since the beginning of the Victorian restoration. An inspection of the fabric had revealed that, by 1952, extensive structural repairs were necessary. Since Scott's restoration of the lantern, death-watch beetle had taken hold and similar problems were in evidence in other roofs. The sum of £60,000 would need to be spent. When the works were completed, as Dean Hankey pointed out, 'the cathedral will look precisely the same as it did twelve months ago'. That this has been the objective of most repair work since then is a tribute to the impact of William Morris's ideas on twentieth-century church restoration. Minimal intervention and self-effacing, traditional repair is part of the philosophy so effectively promoted by his Society for the Protection of Ancient Buildings.

By 1953, money was raised for the reordering of the space behind Scott's high altar (now St Etheldreda's chapel) as a memorial to those from Cambridgeshire who had died in the Second World War. Dykes Bower panelled the east wall using the pilasters of the pre-Victorian organ case which had been stored. This covered up some fragmentary medieval paintings of kings below the east window and Victorian monuments were moved out as the floor was paved with polished Purbeck marble. In the following year Bomber Command of the New Zealand Air Force offered a window as a memorial to their servicemen and those of the RAF who had flown out of local bases, sustaining heavy losses. In 1957 it was installed in the north choir aisle to replace Lusson's 'shocking' window. Coats of arms, the patron saints of both services and scenes of bombers, searchlights and flak-barrages were arranged in a dense pattern of lead work by E. Liddall Armitage for Powells of Whitefriars.

It was in this year that the question of the Victorian windows was revived by the dean. Nothing was done immediately, but in the 1960s certain windows were removed in response to general dissatisfaction with the low light levels in the presbytery. This problem was connected with a prestigious commission for a new high altar cross which Louis Osman was asked to design in 1961. The Goldsmiths' Company, who had offered generous grants to the project, suggested that it should have a figure of Christ in gold by Graham Sutherland, for which they would give additional funds. When the job was finished in 1965 the project was considerably over budget and the cross itself proved too small for so grand a setting (Sutherland's figure was a mere 23 centimetres). Some obscured Victorian glazing was removed from four tribune windows round the site of the shrine in an effort to throw light on the altar but this had the reverse effect. The removal of 'some exceptionally bad glass in a window in the south choir aisle' did, however, succeed in making the great candlesticks visible from the west door for the first time. The cross itself was still invisible even from the chancel. When the cathedral decided that it could no longer accept this diminutive crucifix, the story was pounced on by a national press sensing a Sutherland controversy comparable to the critical reception of his Churchill portrait. The problem was resolved when the cross was bought and all costs met by a wealthy resident of the French Riviera, who wanted it for his private chapel.

Other works of art were more successfully absorbed, including a statue of Etheldreda by Philip Turner (1961, now in St Etheldreda's chapel) and a bronze *Noli me tangere* by David Wynne, which came to the cathedral in 1964. It stands in the south transept in a good relationship with the slender arcades of the tribune walkway *(Fig. 26)*. Hans Feibusch's bronze *Christus* who welcomes visitors and congregations at the west door was acquired in 1980.

LITURGICAL CHANGES

Since the war there have been a number of developments concerned with liturgy. In 1960 a new nave altar was installed, signifying a shift in the liturgical focus. This followed on from proposals to clear the octagon of its dense Victorian pews and experiment with nave worship that were first formulated in 1937. A growing trend away from the Prayer Book offices towards a greater emphasis on the eucharist was given further impetus at the Second Vatican Council of 1962, when the Catholic Church instituted a more accessible form of the mass. It was now to be celebrated in the midst of the people. The powerful effect of this change on Anglicanism is represented by the nave altars that are now found in so many churches. Ely was especially well equipped to cope with this change and the octagon could almost have been designed for the new kind of service. The present arrangements in the octagon were first contemplated in 1970. The stalls for choir and clergy were one of the last works of the architect George Pace, completed in 1978 after his death. The style is very characteristic of him. The design is appropriately understated and the tops of the major seats cleverly evoke the castellated details of the octagon and lantern.

The re-creation of one of the south transept

chapels in 1958 by the removal of the southern bay of the chapter library created a place for private prayer. A simple iron screen was designed by the surveyor, Donovan Purcell, and the east window became home to some of the better fragments of medieval glass. The chapel, dedicated to St Æthelwold and St Dunstan, is also used for the reservation of the Sacrament. Hitherto these functions had been provided by St Edmund's chapel but the increase in the numbers of visitors making their way to the Lady chapel had detracted from its tranquillity. Proposals, current at the time of writing, to rebuild the pilgrims' passage to the Lady chapel from the north presbytery aisle will change the atmosphere of the transept once more. (They will also allow the introduction of adequate conveniences for visitors and congregation, the first serious attempt at such provision since the destruction of the monastic reredorter after the Reformation.)

The site of St Etheldreda's shrine, vacant since the Reformation, was marked in 1969 by an inscribed slab carved by David Kindersley and lit by four candles. Every year in services held on 23 June (her principal feast) and on 17 October (her translation) the whole congregation processes first to Ovin's stone and then to this site.

In 1996 the cathedral was rewired and a new system of lighting introduced. This scheme was devised on the principle of theatre lighting to provide the most effective and natural illumination of the architecture while addressing the need for working light for the congregation, choir and clergy. Capable of a wide range of different settings, it has a liturgical capability seen at its most dramatic in the Advent carol service in which the coming of the light is the central theme.

The use of the cathedral has developed dramatically in the last decade in response to changes in society and in particular the expectations and needs of visitors and the local community. The controversial introduction of a charge for tourists has been emulated by other cathedrals. At Ely it helps to meet running costs and also funds an increasingly ambitious programme of events and educational activities. Sometimes the cathedral swarms with children dressed as monks; and there are lectures, exhibitions and concerts. The annual Christian rock festival for the young people of the diocese may fail to draw the older members of the cathedral congregation, but it causes a clearance of chairs that reveals the nave in its uncluttered Norman splendour. Through activities such as these, the cathedral reaches beyond tourists and its daily round of worship and prayer to a much wider community in a way that would once have been inconceivable.

REPAIRS

In 1939 there had been a certain amount of restoration work in the Lady chapel, where some of the ribs were falling out of the complex vault and where monuments coming away from the wall were relocated. The roofs of the choir and the south transept were dealt with by 1955. In the following year the heavy Norman vault of St Edmund's chapel was taken down and rebuilt. By 1957 the western belfry had been repaired and in 1958 the renewing of the lantern leadwork was nearing completion.

In 1964 stone began to fall from the west face of the Galilee porch, prompting an extensive programme, including the re-carving of several of the capitals and, internally, the replacement of the much-eroded Purbeck marble shafts. This work continued until 1968.

The west tower

Inspection of the west tower in 1971 revealed large quantities of loose masonry and in 1973 the tower was scaffolded for repair. It made a

remarkable sight, enveloped in a network of 45 kilometres of steel tubing. A great deal of work was carried out to the masonry of the octagonal top but the opportunity was also taken to introduce strengthening in the body of the tower.

The tower had been moving ever since it was built by Bishop Ridel after 1174. The main settlement must have halted before 1250 because there are no visible distortions in the walls of the Galilee. The piers had been heavily strengthened in 1405–7. The walls of the main body of the tower, however, showed signs of distress and the main movement was contained in the wall thickness. Here the two outer leaves of masonry surrounding the central rubble core were moving away from one another. Scott's wrought-iron reinforcement, introduced between 1860 and 1871, was intended to counteract this bursting of the walls, but the expansion of his rusting ironwork was cracking the masonry. In 1973 the time had come for a more thorough and efficient system of reinforcement. It was devised by Professor Jacques Heyman, whose engineering advice has guided the work of three successive surveyors to the fabric. The walls were drilled at several levels and a horizontal lattice of short stainless-steel rods was inserted to tie the two separating leaves together. In many places the rubble core had partially disintegrated to leave voids. These were filled by pumping in a grout of Portland cement. Long stainless-steel ties, threaded through the length of the four walls, also stabilised the basic geometry of the tower. Scott's reinforcement – which, according to John Bacon, weighed 100 tons and which blocked the spiral staircases and appeared externally in ugly strapping – could now be removed. The fourteenth-century octagonal

101. (left) The west tower under scaffolding for repairs to the octagonal top and strengthening works in 1973. (Photograph by Hallam Ashley)

top and its turrets were also strengthened with reinforced concrete ring-beams.

The repair of the cathedral will always remain the pressing responsibility of the dean and chapter. The most extensive campaign of restoration this century is only now drawing towards its conclusion. This work has cost £11 million, with £8 million coming from the generosity of local donors and the balance from English Heritage. It began in 1986 when the lead on the nave roof was damaged in severe winds. The roofs of both the main volume and the aisles were completely repaired by 1988 and the painted ceiling of Le Strange and Gambier Parry was cleaned. In 1988–9 the Lady chapel roof and the stonework of its gables were tackled. In 1989/90 the bulging of the upper walls of the south transept was corrected by a grouting and a reinforcing campaign similar to that of the west tower. More gales in 1990 sucked out one of the windows of the lantern, prompting another phase of repair to its windows and leadwork, which was finished in 1991. The repair of the south-west transept was completed in 1993. In 1994 the Prior's Door was enclosed for the first time since the demolition of the cloisters in the seventeenth century and its famous sculpture is now protected from the weather.

Provided the weather is kept out and accidents are avoided, much of the internal fabric will survive for thousands of years. But every century it will be necessary to repair and replace some of the external stonework. The recent stone repair has been guided by a policy of giving priority to those elements such as strings, hood moulds and set-offs which are designed to shed water. Nothing is replaced that remains in serviceable condition and retains its shape. The work begins with a stone-by-stone survey and, as it progresses, it is carefully monitored and recorded by archaeologists. Developing archaeological techniques and new methods of recording have revealed a great deal about the history of the building and have provided

141

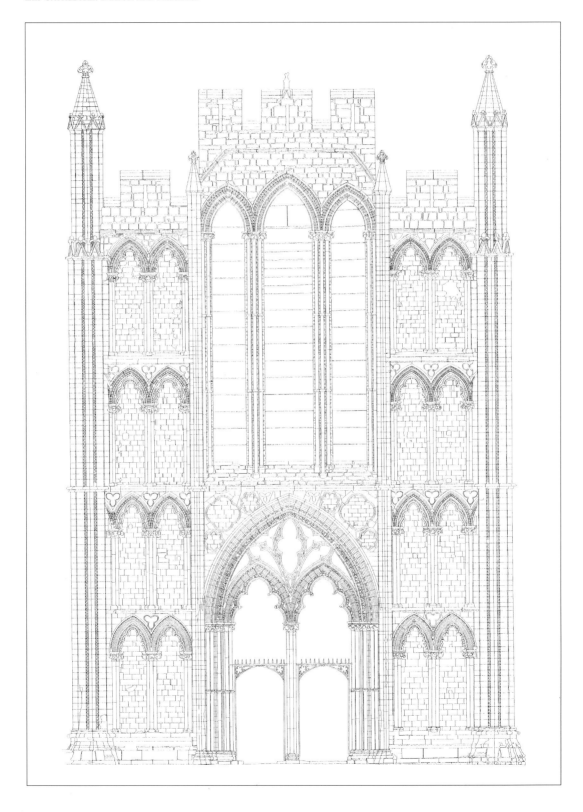

the sort of detailed data from which future archaeologists will be able to draw their own conclusions *(Col. pl. 18)*.

The repair of the south side of the choir and presbytery was begun in 1993 and finished in 1996. The south side of the octagon followed on from this work and scaffolding was soon going up around the north side of the choir and presbytery. As vertical sections of the scaffolding have been removed to reveal the eastern end of the presbytery, restored and cleaned, others have been erected to engulf the north side of the octagon and the east face of the north transept.

In the last few years no visitor to the cathedral has seen the building without some major element concealed by repair scaffolding. Even as we approach the third millennium, there is one more campaign of work to be undertaken, on the Galilee porch. This activity is frustrating for photographers but, as we have seen, there have been very few periods in the history of the building when major work was not under way. It is through the perpetual process of repair that great historical buildings continue to live and to sustain the remarkable levels of craftsmanship for which we value them so highly. The technique of cutting and laying masonry has not changed significantly since the thirteenth century. Timber still needs to be sawn and jointed by the traditional methods and lead is still used in the old way. The few modern innovations are only used to give strength to the old fabric where it cannot be provided in other ways.

In our century of change the cathedral has come to represent for many people a symbol of the things that they value, an emblem of endurance and something good in a troubled world. We have seen, however, that its past embraces every aspect of human ambition and behaviour. It has rarely been static and has often attracted controversy and radical change, and sometimes violence. It bears all the signs and scars of this eventful history and part of the purpose of this book has been to show how this evidence might be read and understood on its own terms.

102. The west front of the Galilee drawn by photogrammetry in 1999. These drawings, whose accuracy and detail far exceed the hand-measured surveys of the past, provide posterity with a detailed record and greatly assist in the planning and documenting of masonry repairs. (Plowman Craven)

Rev: Viri Decan: & Capit:
Hujus Eccl: Cathedral:
Tabellam hanc delineand:
& in ære incidend: Curaverunt

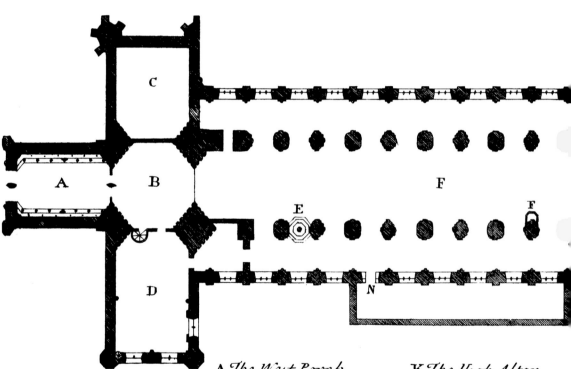

PLAN 2

The plan of the cathedral from Browne Willis, A Survey of the Cathedrals of Lincoln, Ely, Oxford and Peterborough, 1730, shows the building before the choir was moved from the crossing as well as the early positions of significant tombs.

A The West Porch
B The West Tower
C The ruined part of the Gallilee
D The South Gallilee now the Church Work house
E The Font
F F The nave of the Church where the Sermons are preacht & pulpit
G The Choir entrance under ye stone Gallery where ye Organs stands
H The Choir which has 35 stalls on each side
I The Circumference of the Lantern or Middle Tower

K The High Altar
L The North Cross Isle and Door
M The Lady Chapell now Trinity parish Church
N The doors into the Cloysters which are ruined
O The Vestreys
PP The Dean & Prebenda...
Q The Archive Room
R The Library
S The presbytery an... Old Altar place

of the Cathedral
of Ely.

M

L

L

I

H

K

S

P

P

Q

O

O

R

N

I

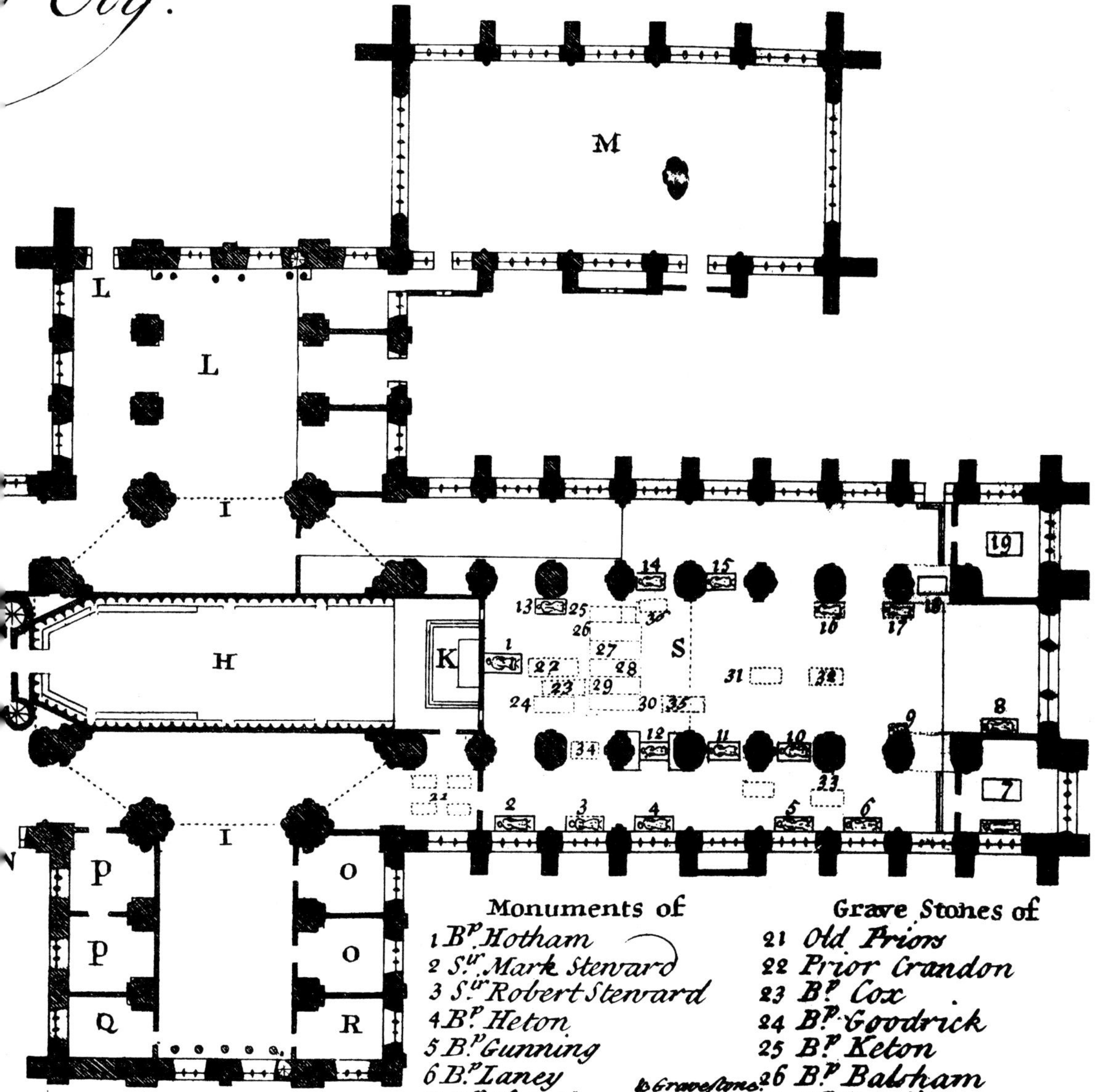

Monuments of

1 B.ᵖ Hotham
2 S.ⁱʳ Mark Steward
3 S.ⁱʳ Robert Steward
4 B.ᵖ Heton
5 B.ᵖ Gunning
6 B.ᵖ Laney
7 B.ᵖ West Chapell Tomb
8 B.ᵖ Lusborough
9 B.ᵖ Fleetwood
10 Tiptoft Earl of Worcester
11 B.ᵖ Barnet
12 B.ᵖ Will: Luda
13 Dean Cæsar
14 B.ᵖ Redman
15 B.ᵖ Kilkenny
16 B.ᵖ Patrick
17 B.ᵖ Moor
18 B.ᵖ Gray
19 B.ᵖ Alcocks Chapell.
& gravestone

Grave Stones of

21 Old Priors
22 Prior Crandon
23 B.ᵖ Cox
24 B.ᵖ Goodrick
25 B.ᵖ Keton
26 B.ᵖ Balsham
27 B.ᵖ Fontibus
28 B.ᵖ Walpole
29 B.ᵖ Orford
30 Dean Tindal
31 S.ʳ Will: Thorp
32 B.ᵖ Norvold
33 Prebendary Nalson
34 Dean Steward
35 Dean Bell
36 Dean Moss

b gravestone

rey
ter-House

A Scale of Feet
20 30 40 50 60 70 80 90 100

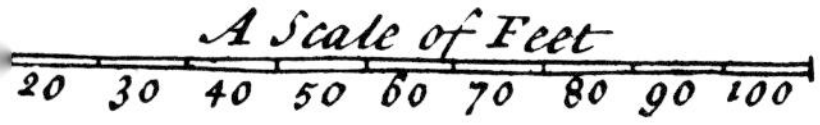

BIBLIOGRAPHY

GENERAL WORKS

H. Wharton, *Anglia Sacra*, 1691

B. Willis, *A Survey of the Cathedrals of Lincoln, Ely, Oxford and Peterborough*, 1730

J. Bentham, *The History and Antiquities of the Cathedral and Conventual Church of Ely*, 2nd edition with a supplement by W. Stevenson, 1812

J. Britton, *The Architectural Antiquities of Great Britain*, Vol. 5, 1826

G. Millers, *A Description of the Cathedral Church of Ely with some account of the Conventual Buildings*, 3rd edition, 1834

D.J. Stewart, *On the Architectural History of Ely Cathedral*, 1868

G.G. Scott, 'Ely Cathedral', in Charles Merivale, (ed.), *Summary of the Proceedings at the Bisextenary Festival of St Etheldreda at Ely*, 1873

C.W. Stubbs, *Historical Memorials of Ely Cathedral*, 1897

C.W. Stubbs, *Ely Cathedral Handbook*, 21st edition, 1904

E.R. Chapman, *The Sacrist Rolls of Ely*, 1907

E. Miller, *The Abbey and Bishopric of Ely*, 1951

R.B. Pugh (ed.), *The Victoria History of the County of Cambridge and the Isle of Ely*, Vol. 4, 1953

E.O. Blake (ed.), *Liber Eliensis*, Camden third series, XCII, 1962

N. Pevsner, *The Buildings of England: Cambridgeshire*, 2nd edition, 1970

P. Moore, *The Three Restorations of Ely Cathedral*, 1973

D. Owen, *The Library and Muniments of Ely Cathedral*, 1973

D. Purcell, *The Building of Ely Cathedral*, 1973

G. Cobb, *English Cathedrals: The Forgotten Centuries*, 1980

J.H. Harvey, *English Medieval Architects: A Biographical Dictionary down to 1550*, 2nd edition, 1984

P. Blakeman, *The Book of Ely*, 1990

D.M. Collins, 'The Fabric Archives of Ely Cathedral and College from the Commonwealth to 1993', unpublished report commissioned by the dean and chapter, 1994

CHAPTER 1

D.H. Farmer (ed.), *Bede: Ecclesiastical History of the English People*, 1990

D.H. Farmer, *The Oxford Dictionary of Saints*, 1992

H.C. Darby, *The Medieval Fenland*, 1974

James Campbell (ed.), *The Anglo-Saxons*, 1991

M. Lapidge (ed.), *The Blackwell Encyclopaedia of Anglo-Saxon England*, 1999

N. Sneesby, *Etheldreda: Princess, Queen, Abbess and Saint*, 1999

J. Coles and D. Hall, *Changing Landscapes: the Ancient Fenland*, 1998

E. Okasha, *Anglo-Saxon Non Runic Inscriptions*, 1971

D. Scragg (ed.), *The Battle of Maldon AD 991*, 1991

F. Wormald, *The Benedictional of St Ethelwold*, 1959

M. Swanton, *Anglo-Saxon Prose*, 1993

D. Whitelock, *The Anglo-Saxon Chronicle, a revised translation*, 1961

C.R. Dodwell, *Anglo-Saxon Art: A New Perspective*, 1982

E. Fernie, *The Architecture of the Anglo-Saxons*, 1983

CHAPTERS 2 AND 3

E. Fernie, 'Observations on the Norman Plan of Ely Cathedral', *Medieval Art and Architecture at Ely Cathedral*, 1979, 1–7

S. Ferguson, 'The Romanesque Cathedral at Ely: an Archaeological Evaluation of its Construction', unpublished PhD thesis, University of Columbia, 1986

K.J. Conant, *Carolingian and Romanesque Architecture 800–1200*, 1978

J. Crook, 'The Romanesque East Arm and Crypt of Winchester Cathedral', *Journal of the British Archaeological Association*, CXLII, 1989, 1–36

J.P. McAleer, 'A Note about the Transept Cross Aisles of Ely Cathedral', *Proceedings of the Cambridgeshire Antiquarian Society*, LXXXI, 1992

J.P. McAleer, 'Some Observations about the Romanesque Choir of Ely Cathedral', *Journal of the Society of Architectural Historians*, 53, 1994, 80–94

B. Cherry, 'Romanesque Architecture in Eastern England', *Journal of the British Archaeological Association*, CXXXI, 1978, 1–29

C. Hart, *The Thorney Annals 963–1412 AD*, 1997

G. Simpson, 'Ely Cathedral – The Nave Roof', unpublished University of Nottingham archaeological report prepared for the dean and chapter, 1996

A. Gransden (ed.), *Bury St Edmunds: Medieval Art, Architecture, Archaeology and Economy*, 1998 (includes articles by E. Fernie, S. Heywood and P. McAleer on the Romanesque abbey church at Bury St Edmunds)

K. Fearn, 'Ely Cathedral. Masons' Marks in the South-west Transept', unpublished MA thesis, University of Nottingham, 1993

K. Fearn, P. Marshall and G. Simpson, 'The South-west Transept of Ely Cathedral',

unpublished University of Nottingham archaeological report prepared for the dean and chapter, 1995

G. Zarnecki, *The Early Sculpture of Ely Cathedral*, 1958

W.H. St John Hope, 'Quire Screens in English Churches with special reference to the Twelfth-century Quire Screen formerly in the Cathedral Church at Ely', *Archaeologia*, 68, 1916–17, 43–110

A. Klukas, 'Alteria Superiora: The Function and Significance of the Tribune Chapel in Anglo-Norman Romanesque; a Problem in the Relationship of Liturgical Requirements and Architectural Form', unpublished PhD thesis, University of Pittsburgh, 1978

T. Symons (ed.), *Regularis Concordia*, 1953

D. Knowles (ed.), *The Monastic Constitutions of Lanfranc*, 1951

CHAPTER 4

P. Draper, 'Bishop Northwold and the Cult of St Etheldreda', *Medieval Art and Architecture at Ely Cathedral*, 1979, 8–27

M. Roberts, 'The Effigy of Bishop Hugh de Northwold in Ely Cathedral', *Burlington Magazine*, CXXX, 1988, 77–84

Christopher Wilson, *The Gothic Cathedral*, 1992

J. Heyman, *The Stone Skeleton*, 1995

J.M. Neale and B. Webb, *The Symbolism of Churches and Church Ornaments; a Translation of the Rationale Divinorum Officiorum, written by W. Durandus*, 1893

M.R. James, *The Apocalypse in Art*, 1931

A.G. and W.O. Hassall, *The Douce Apocalypse*, 1961

E. Panofsky, *Abbot Suger on the Abbey Church of St Denis and its Art Treasures*, 1979

L. Reilly, *An Architectural History of Peterborough Cathedral*, 1997

F.E. Warren, *The Sarum Missal in English*, 1913

V. Pritchard, *English Medieval Graffiti*, 1967

P.G. Lindley, 'The Tomb of Bishop William de Luda: An Architectural Model at Ely Cathedral', *Proceedings of the Cambridge Antiquarian Society*, LXXII, 1984, 75–87

Chapter 5

P.G. Lindley, 'The Monastic Cathedral at Ely *c.*1320–*c.*1350: Art and Patronage in Medieval East Anglia', unpublished PhD thesis, University of Cambridge, 1985

P.G. Lindley, 'The Imagery of the Octagon at Ely', *Journal of the British Archaeological Association,* CXXXIX, 1986, 74–99

C.W. Wilson, 'The Origins of the Perpendicular Style and its Development to *c.*1360', unpublished PhD thesis, University of London, 1980

C. Hewett, *English Cathedral and Monastic Carpentry,* 1985

J. Heyman and E.C. Wade, 'The Timber Octagon of Ely Cathedral', *Proceedings of the Institute of Civil Engineers,* 1985, 78, Part 1, 1421–1436

K. Fearn, 'Medieval and Later Woodwork in the Choir of Ely Cathedral', *Journal of the British Archaeological Association,* CL, 1997, 59–75

C. Grössinger, *The World Upside Down: English Misericords,* 1997

M.R. James, *The Sculptures in the Lady Chapel at Ely,* 1895

N. Coldstream, 'Ely Cathedral: The Fourteenth-Century Work', *Medieval Art and Architecture at Ely,* 1979, 28–46

N. Coldstream, 'The Lady Chapel at Ely: Its place in the English Decorated Style', *East Anglian and other studies presented to Barbara Dodwell,* Reading Medieval Studies XI, 1985

N. Coldstream, *The Decorated Style,* 1994

J. Bony, *The English Decorated Style,* 1979

P. Dixon and J. Heward, 'A Report on the Lady Chapel Bridge, Ely', unpublished archaeological report prepared for the dean and chapter, 1999

L. Keen, 'Fourteenth-century Tile Pavements in Prior Crauden's Chapel and in the South Transept', *Medieval Art and Architecture at Ely Cathedral,* 1979, 47–57

P. Binski and D. Park, 'A Ducciesque Episode at Ely: The Mural Decoration of Prior Crauden's Chapel', *England in the Fourteenth Century. Proceedings of the 1985 Harlaxton Symposium,* 1987

Chapter 6

T.D. Atkinson, *An Architectural History of the Benedictine Monastery of St Etheldreda at Ely,* Cambridge, 1933

S.I. Ladds, *The Monastery of Ely,* 1930

Abbot Parry OSB and E. de Waal, *The Rule of St Benedict,* 1990

A. Holton-Krayenbuhl, *The Benedictine Monastery of Medieval Ely,* 1998

A. Holton-Krayenbuhl, 'The Infirmary Complex at Ely', *Archaeological Journal,* 154, 1997, 118–72

T. Cocke, A. Holton-Krayenbuhl and T. Malim, 'Ely Cathedral precincts: The North Range', *Proceedings of the Cambridgeshire Antiquarian Society,* 78, 1989

J. Fletcher, 'Medieval Timberwork at Ely', *Medieval Art and Architecture at Ely Cathedral,* 1979

J. Fletcher and F.W.M. Haslop, 'The West Range at Ely and its Romanesque Roof', *Archaeological Journal,* CXXVI, 1969, 171–6

B. Harvey, *Living and Dying in England, 1100–1540: The Monastic Experience,* 1993

D. Sherlock, *Signs for Silence,* 1992

R. Sharpe, S.P. Carly, R.M. Thomson and A.G. Watson, *English Benedictine Libraries: The Shorter Catalogue,* 1996

Chapter 7

F. Woodman, 'The Vault of Ely Lady Chapel: Fourteenth or Fifteenth Century?', *Gesta,* 23, Part 2, 1984

J. Fletcher, 'Four Scenes from the Life of St Etheldreda', *Antiquaries Journal,* LIV, 1974, 287–9

P. Lasko and N.J. Morgan (eds.), *Medieval Art in East Anglia,* 1973

J.H. Harvey, *The Perpendicular Style,* 1978

G.H. Cook, *Medieval Chantries and Chantry Chapels,* 1947

W.C. Leedy, *Fan Vaulting: A Study of Form, Technology and Meaning,* 1980

E. Duffy, *The Stripping of the Altars,* 1992

CHAPTER 8

J. Phillips, *The Reformation of Images: Destruction of Art in England, 1535–1660*, 1973
J. Foxe, *Actes and Monuments*, 1563 ('Book of Martyrs')
B.M.G. Smedley, *Holy Trinity, Ely: In Search of a Vanished Parish*, 1998
S.E. Lehmberg, *The Reformation of Cathedrals: Cathedrals in English Society, 1485–1603*, 1988
D.J. Stewart, 'The Distribution of Buildings of the Dissolved Monastery at Ely', *Archaeological Journal*, LIV, 1897, 174–85

CHAPTER 9

T. Carlyle, *Oliver Cromwell's Letters and Speeches*, 2nd edition, 1893
C. Hill, *God's Englishman*, 1970
R. Holmes, *Cromwell's Ely*, 1975
S.E. Lehmberg, *Cathedrals under Siege: Cathedrals in English Society 1600–1700*, 1996
E. Wickham-Legg (ed.), *A Relation of a Short Survey of the Western Counties ...*, Camden Miscellany, XVI, 1936
C. Morris (ed.), *The Journeys of Celia Fiennes*, 1949
William Dugdale, *Monasticon Anglicanum*, 1655

CHAPTER 10

T. Cocke, 'The Architectural History of Ely Cathedral from 1540–1840', *Medieval Art and Architecture at Ely Cathedral*, 1979, 71–8
T. Cocke, *The Ingenious Mr Essex, Architect (catalogue of a Bicentenary Exhibition at the Fitzwilliam Museum, Cambridge)*, 1984
T. Cocke, 'The "Old Conventual Church" at Ely, A False Trail in Romanesque Studies', *Art and Patronage in the English Romanesque*, eds. S. Macready and F.H. Thompson, Society of Antiquaries Occasional Papers (N.S.), viii, 1986, 77–86
S.F. Baylis, 'The Most Untractable of All Saxon Uncouthness: Eighteenth-Century Painted Glass in Ely Cathedral and the Removal of the Choir', *Antiquaries Journal*, 68, 1988, 99–114

CHAPTER 11

C. Johnson, *An Account of the Trials and Execution of the Ely and Littleport Rioters in 1816*, 1893
W. Cobbett, *Rural Rides in Surrey, Kent and other Counties*, 1853
A.W.N. Pugin, *Contrasts or a Parallel between the Noble Edifices of the Middle Ages and the Corresponding Buildings of the Present Day shewing the Present Decay of Taste*, 1836
J.W. Bacon, *A Record of the Restorations, Repairs etc. done in and about Ely Cathedral since 1818. Prepared by J.W. Bacon, Clerk of Works 1871*, Cambridge University Library, Ely Dean and Chapter, MS 37
R.R. Rowe, 'The Octagon and Lantern of Ely Cathedral', *Royal Institute of British Architects Sessional Papers*, I, 1875–6
George Gilbert Scott, *Personal and Professional Recollections* (1879), ed. G. Stamp, 1995
H. Goodwin, *Ely Gossip*, 1892
P. Moore, *The Stained Glass of Ely Cathedral*, 1973
W.M. Jacob, 'Henry Styleman le Strange: Tractarian, Artist, Squire', in *The Church and the Arts*, ed. D. Wood, 1992
D. Farr (ed.), *Thomas Gambier Parry 1816–1888 as Artist and Collector*, 1993
P.G. Lindley, '"Carpenter's Gothic" and Gothic Carpentry: Contrasting Attitudes to the Restoration of the Octagon at Ely', *Architectural History*, 30, 1987, 83–112

CHAPTER 12

J. Heyman, 'The Strengthening of the West Tower of Ely Cathedral', *Proceedings of the Institute of Civil Engineers*, 60, Part 1, 1976, 123–47
S. Gee (ed.), *Caring for our Past: Building for the Future. An important chapter in the history of Ely Cathedral*, 1992

INDEX

Page numbers in *italic* are references to black-and-white illustrations.
References to the colour plates (between pp. 24 and 25 and pp. 120 and 121) are shown in **bold**.